THE QUOTABLE TOZER

The Quotable Tozer

WISE WORDS WITH A PROPHETIC EDGE

Compiled by Harry Verploegh

Biography by
Virginia Verploegh Steinmetz

CHRISTIAN PUBLICATIONS
CAMP HILL, PENNSYLVANIA

Christian Publications, Inc.
3825 Hartzdale Drive, Camp Hill, PA 17011
www.cpi-horizon.com

Faithful, biblical publishing since 1883

ISBN: 0-87509-546-1
LOC Catalog Card Number: 84-70413

© 1984 by Harry Verploegh
Original published as A.W. Tozer:
An Anthology ©1984 by Harry Verploegh

Grateful acknowledgment is made to
Harper and Row for permission to quote from
The Knowledge of the Holy, © 1961

98   99   00   01   02   7   6   5   4   3

Cover portrait by Karl Foster

FAIR USE INFORMATION

Christian Publications gives permission for all quotes in this book—with the exception of those from *The Knowledge of the Holy*, which is copyrighted by Harper-Collins—to be used in published material under the following conditions:

1. The quotations must not exceed five percent of the content of the published material.

2. A credit line such as the following must be printed either after the quote or as a footnote or on a permissions page (replace bracketed words with the appropriate book title, date and page number)·

   From [book title] by A.W. Tozer, copyright [copyright year] by Christian Publications, page [page number]. Used with permission.

If use beyond what is allowed here is desired, please contact the permissions editor, Christian Publications, 3825 Hartzdale Drive, Camp Hill, PA 17011.

This book is
affectionately
dedicated
to the
A.W. Tozer
family

Contents

Preface

*A*lmost anyone can compile an anthology like this. You simply read the works of an author, choose what appeals to you and publish it. However, having a personal association with the author and sensing what was in his mind helps give credence to any representative selection.

While A.W. Tozer was pastor of the Southside Alliance Church in Chicago, he once presented me with a small book titled *A Guide to True Peace, or The Excellency of Inward and Spiritual Prayer*, selections compiled chiefly from the writing of Fénelon, Guyon and Molinos. According to A.B. Simpson this same little book, given to him by a friend, became one of the turning points of his life. I have it yet, after perhaps forty years. The flyleaf bears this inscription in Tozer's hand:

*To my friend
Harry Verploegh.
A. W. Tozer*

I do not remember the occasion that prompted the gift, but I want to think that he considered me a kindred soul, having appreciation for his thought and ministry. I am proud and honored to have been his friend.

I knew A.W. Tozer well, having heard him preach week after week for thirty years, often kneeling with him in prayer, serving with him on church committees, working with him while he was editor of *The Alliance Witness*, playing golf or baseball or breaking bread with him (usually a sandwich and a malted milk at the corner drugstore), chauffeuring him on many occasions, and having fellowship with him for almost all of the years of his Chicago pastorate. When we were away from him, we called him "Tozer." In his presence we said "Mr. Tozer," never "Reverend" or "Doctor Tozer." Titles seemed to embarrass him, to make him feel uneasy, as though he wasn't considered one of the people. He must have had weaknesses; we all do. But I found no fault in him. Someone has said, "Great men are very apt to have great faults, and the faults appear the greater by their contrast with their excellencies." Tozer was very much a part of my life, and I treasure the memory of this good and dedicated man.

Oswald Chambers wrote, "God speaks to us, not by visions and dreams, but by words." A.W. Tozer had a way with words, and they speak as plainly and truly to me today as they did a generation ago. This collection of excerpts from his works is the result of favorable reader response to the A.W. Tozer anthology currently appearing in *The Alliance Life*. It is my hope that Tozer's words will speak to the reader as they have spoken to me, perhaps prompting closer examination of the books from which these quotations have been selected.

A Biographical Sketch

*A*iden Wilson Tozer described himself as an "ignorant seventeen-year-old boy" when he began to listen to preaching on the streets of Akron, Ohio, and responded to Christ's invitation "come unto me all ye that labor." *Find rest, learn my yoke, know lowliness of heart.* Tozer had learned the meaning of labor as the third of six children growing up on the family farm in mountainous Newburg (formerly La Jose), Pennsylvania, near Mahaffey. When Zene, his eldest brother, left the farm around 1907 to work for the Goodrich Rubber Company in Akron, the ten-year-old Aiden did the work of a hired hand and later remarked on his large "ungifted hands," which had done a lot of farm work as a boy.

Although Tozer did not have the advantage of formal education beyond the grammar grades at Wood School, his grandmother taught him what she knew and seemed to have sparked his interest in spiritual realities with her daily habit of consulting a dream book for clues to the significance of objects she had seen in her dreams. On Sundays Tozer read what books were available on the farm. Later when he took a job selling candy, peanuts and books as a "butcher boy" on the Vicksburg and Pacific Railroad, he recalled that he had not made enough money on the job because he preferred to "sit and read the books from Vicksburg to the end of the line."

After his conversion to Christ, Tozer would withdraw from the constant activity in his Akron home, where his parents took in boarders, to quiet sanctuaries in the attic and basement. There he began his warfare in prayer and an eager search for spiritual realities through the study of Scripture, of theology, of literature, of history, and began to respond to the "fluidity and fullness" of the English language as an instrument for articulating the soul's discovery of God.

The adolescent Tozer's new faith had little nurturing in his own family circle, where no one at that time was a believer, but he joined Grace Methodist Church in Akron and was baptized by immersion in the Church of the Brethren. Determined to obey a call to preach despite his lack of training, he was encouraged in this purpose by Reverend S.M. Gerow, pastor of the Locust Street Christian and Missionary Alliance Church, and became a member of Gerow's congregation. It was at this time that he met Ada Pfautz, whom he married in 1918 when he was twenty-one. It was Ada's saintly mother, who, with Gerow, nurtured him in the early years of the Christian life by lending him religious books and acquainting him with her work as a home missionary in the Pentecostal church.

Two years after his marriage, Tozer was ordained as an Alliance minister at Beulah Beach, Ohio, and he and Ada moved to his first charge in Nutter Fort, West Virginia. On the occasion of his ordination, Tozer wrote a prayer of dedication. In it he accepted the honor of a high and holy calling, but at the same time he took on Christ's yoke of discipline and determined to learn lowliness of heart. Tozer's sense of the sublime and the humble aspects of his call are well expressed in the title he later gave to this prayer when he printed it in *The Alliance Weekly* during his first year as editor. He called his ordination vow "The Prayer of a Minor Prophet."

Lord Jesus, I come to Thee for spiritual preparation. Lay Thy hand upon me. Anoint me with the oil of the New Testament prophet. Forbid that I should become a religious scribe and thus lose my prophetic calling. Save me from the curse that lies dark across the face of the modern clergy, the curse of compromise, of imitation, of professionalism. Save me from the error of judging a church by its size, its popularity or the amount of its yearly offering. Help me to remember that I am a prophet, not a promoter, not a religious manager—but a prophet. Let me never become a slave to crowds. Heal my soul from bondage to things. Let me not waste my days puttering around the house. Lay Thy terror upon me, O God, and drive me to the place of prayer where I may wrestle with principalities and powers and the rulers of the darkness of this world. Deliver me from overeating and late sleeping. Teach me self-discipline that I may be a good soldier of Jesus Christ.

Tozer's dedication as a young pastor to a life of strenuous self-education and courageous resistance to the clerical temptations of compromise, imitations and slick professionalism marked his distinctive ministry of forty-three years—though with characteristic honesty he once said that his spiritual progress had not always been a straightforward but a "zigzag course to heaven." The yoke of Christ, of discipline, which he was called to bear, was not so much the discipline of physical or mental suffering, of pioneer mission work, of persecution, but of spiritual and intellectual preparation for the preaching and teaching ministry. Tozer's yoke was to learn the disciplines of thinking, reading and writing in the service of Christ, of The Christian and Missionary Alliance, and eventually of evangelical Protestants worldwide.

He demonstrated the godly exercise of his gifts in the consistently penetrating quality of his preaching during his pastorates at the Southside Alliance Church in Chicago (1928-1959) and the Avenue Road Church of The Christian and Missionary Alliance in Toronto (1959-1963), in his books of pastoral theology such as *The Pursuit of God* (1948), *The Divine Conquest* (1950) and *The Knowledge of the Holy* (1961); in his biographies of A.B. Simpson (*Wingspread*, 1942) and Robert A. Jaffray (*Let My People Go*, 1947), in his articles for religious periodicals, his radio talks, his guest preaching series, his high literacy and graphic standards for *The Alliance Witness* and in his influential editorials in that periodical during his tenure as editor from 1950 until his death in 1963.

From the earliest days of his ministry, Tozer was convinced that to be an effective preacher of the Word, he had to develop sensitivity and precision in the use of words. He listened to other preachers and kept a notebook of their clichés. Dead language, powerless to rouse the spiritually dead, was his enemy. After he became editor of *The Alliance Witness*, Tozer issued to those who wrote articles an "index prohibitorum" to protect the periodical from cliché-ridden religious language.

By the time he came to the Chicago church, he realized that he could not use his voice indiscriminately. According to Raymond McAfee, his assistant and choir director during those years, Tozer would place a large volume of Milton's *Paradise Lost* on a music stand and practice modulating his voice by reading the poem aloud. Instead of shouting, he learned to build climactic sentences that would snap and ring, his slight frame rising on tip-toe to match the inflections of his voice.

Tozer kept a spiral notebook in which he copied excerpts from his reading and comments on these passages. The classic English prose writers and poets were his delight. He would regale McAfee or others who provided transportation to meetings with readings from his favorites. His verbal imagination was rich in colorful, sometimes grotesque images and metaphors, which enabled his hearers to see, feel, taste and smell with concrete vividness. In his mouth and in his pen, language was a lively instrument, sometimes exercised playfully in the creative moment, but ever accompanied with the gift of wisdom and spiritual discernment.

Beyond the discipline of his ability to articulate Christian truth, however, was the discipline of those persistent, prophetic emphases by which his ministry is remembered and revered:

—on the worship and knowledge of God,
—on the imperative of unceasing witness to God's grace through world wide mission,
—on the necessity of courageous criticism of religious practices which would erode the centrality of the person of Christ or make religion a form of entertainment,
—on the power of the Holy Spirit to bring men and women into intimacy with God,
—on the importance of wide reading and the value of absorbing and memorizing Scripture, the classical Christian writers (especially the mystics), and the hymnodists.

Those who heard him preach will recognize the salty eloquence of his reproving voice in this attack on gospel ballad singing:

Gospel ballad singing is now quite the rage in the lower echelon of the entertainment world. Many of the shows beamed toward the paying

masses are made acceptable to the religiously
inclined by the introduction of a bit of tongue-in-
cheek religion, usually expressed in these highly
spiced gospel ballads whose theology is a mixture
of paganism and old wives' tales and whose
prevailing mood is one of weak self-pity. Such
holy men as Elijah, Daniel, Ezekiel and John are
turned into burnt-cork minstrels who are made to
preach and prophecy for laughs. . . . Every word
of Christ, every act, was simple, sincere, and dignified. The entire New Testament breathes the
same spirit. . . . It is significant that the two
greatest movements within the church since Pentecost, the sixteenth century Reformation and the
Wesley revival, were characterized by sobriety
and sincerity. They both reached the roots of
society and touched the masses, yet they never
descended to be common or to pander to carnal
flesh. The quality of their preaching was lofty,
serious and dignified, and their singing the same.

While Tozer might have given more attention to the
failure of evangelicals to minister to the lower classes, the
marginal peoples of American society, he saw plainly that
in their desire to make their gospel respectable and ap-
pealing to the rich and powerful, they were creating a
Christianity of the bourgeoisie:

The well-to-do, the upper middle classes, the
politically prominent, the celebrities are accepting our religion by the thousands and parking
their expensive cars outside our church doors, to
the uncontrollable glee of our religious leaders,
who seem completely blind to the fact that the
vast majority of these new patrons of the Lord of

glory have not altered their moral habits in the slightest or given any evidence of true conversion that would have been accepted by the saintly fathers who built the churches.

Despite the wide range of his knowledge of Scripture, theology, history, philosophy and literature, and the recognition given him by individuals and institutions for his intellectual and spiritual stewardship (Wheaton College and Houghton College awarded him honorary doctorates), Tozer was a self-effacing man. When asked to write an article of advice to Christians on books and reading, he began:

My friends no doubt overestimate my ability to speak wisely on this matter, but in the hope that I may be able to contribute somewhat to the spiritual progress of younger and inexperienced Christians I offer a few words of counsel.

His awareness of the danger of being overestimated by others was an endearing quality about A.W. Tozer. David J. Fant tells us in his study of Tozer's ministry, *A.W. Tozer: A Twentieth Century Prophet*, that when guests came to his parents' home "he would flee out of doors or retreat to the kitchen and if possible eat alone." Lowliness of heart did not have to be learned when his circle of influence was small, but as it increased, he knew his humility would be subject to severe tests.

A member of his Chicago congregation and a friend, Isabel Anderson Chase, remembers how hesitant he was to accept a call to that congregation. He failed to respond at first to the formal invitation of the board and had to be pursued. After Tozer accepted this call, he found it difficult to fulfill the expectations of the congregation as a pastoral visitor to their sick, but on one particular occasion when he brought communion to a woman desperately ill, Isabel Chase remembers that "the room was hallowed by the presence of the Lord." Tozer found it easy, however, to communicate with babies. He and Ada raised seven children and supported another child through an agency. On one occasion during the Depression after he had visited a needy family in the neighborhood of the Chicago church, he asked members of the congregation to have milk delivered to this home for the children's sake.

Though Tozer's wife assumed the primary responsibility for raising their children, he particularly enjoyed walking to the park with his city-bred youngsters and sharing the lore he knew about trees and birds. Tozer did not follow his children's education closely, but they were expected to do excellent work and develop their God-given talents to the maximum. Because he believed that hothouse Christians tended to be vulnerable and weak, he allowed three of his sons to attend the University of Chicago, where they would develop strength by exposure to many viewpoints. When his children matured, he enjoyed joshing and debating with them. Wendell Tozer recalls that when he lived at home after college, his father would get up early to make his breakfast so they would have maximum bantering time. Occasionally, Wendell reports,

> he would ask my opinion of a book he liked, and if I didn't agree with him that it was a good book, he would say, "When a book and a head come in contact and there is a hollow sound, you can't conclude that the book is empty."

Those who knew him well believe that Tozer's sense of humor was at least one key to his personality. He was a shy and introverted man. His humor was a means of reaching out to others. It was the necessary ballast in the character of a man in pursuit of God.

In his struggle to maintain spiritual integrity, Tozer demonstrated lowliness of heart despite his widening influence in evangelical circles. He was embarrassed if someone did him a special kindness. He was known to accept preaching engagements without remuneration and cared little about money. He once wrote:

> Any of us who have experienced a life and ministry of faith can tell how the Lord has met our needs. My wife and I would probably have starved in those early years of ministry if we couldn't have trusted God completely for food and everything else. Of course, we believe that God can send money to His believing children— but it becomes a pretty cheap thing to get excited about the money and fail to give the glory to Him who is the Giver!

About His possessions he said:

> If I should make out my will, I would have to leave my books to someone. I have a little household furniture, but not too much and not too expensive. With the books, that would be about all.

Having few material possessions, Tozer nevertheless possessed what was most needful for ministry. In his words:

> I was nineteen years old, earnestly in prayer, kneeling in the front room of my mother-in-law's

home, when I was baptized with a mighty infusion of the Holy Ghost. . . . I know with assurance what God did for me and within me and that nothing on the outside held any important meaning. In desperation, and in faith, I took that leap away from everything that was unimportant to that which was most important—to be possessed by the Spirit of the Living God!

Any tiny work that God has ever done through me and through my ministry for Him dates back to that hour when I was filled with the Spirit. That is why I plead for the spiritual life of the Body of Christ and the eternal ministries of the Eternal Spirit through God's children—His instruments.

In one of his sermons as a seasoned prophet, Tozer asked his congregation to pray that he would experience undiminished spiritual power to labor and to bear the yoke of Christ in lowliness of heart to the end:

Pray for me in the light of the pressures of our times. Pray that I will not just come to a wearied end—an exhausted, tired old preacher, interested only in hunting a place to roost. Pray that I will be willing to let my Christian experience and Christian standards cost me something right down to the last gasp!

Virginia Verploegh Steinmetz
Durham, North Carolina

The righteous need no tombstones;
Their words are their monuments.

TALMUD, *Persahim*, 119a

Activity

We now demand glamour and fast flowing dramatic action. A generation of Christians reared among push buttons and automatic machines is impatient of slower and less direct methods of reaching their goals. We have been trying to apply machine-age methods to our relations with God. We read our chapter, have our short devotions and rush away, hoping to make up for our deep inward bankruptcy by attending another gospel meeting or listening to another thrilling story told by a religious adventurer lately returned from afar.

The tragic results of this spirit are all about us. Shallow lives, hollow religious philosophies, the preponderance of the element of fun in gospel meetings, the glorification of men, trust in religious externalities, quasi-religious fellowships, salesmanship methods, the mistaking of dynamic personality for the power of the Spirit: these and such as these are the symptoms of an evil disease, a deep and serious malady of the soul. [A67]*

Be concerned not with what you have accomplished but over what you might have accomplished if you had followed the Lord completely. [C29]

In this world men are judged by their ability to do. [D55]

. . . there is a lot of religious activity among us. Interchurch basketball tournaments, religious splash parties followed by devotions, weekend camping trips with a Bible quiz around the fire, Sunday school picnics, building fund drives and ministerial breakfasts are with us in unbelievable numbers, and they are carried on with typical American gusto. It is when we enter the sacred precincts of the heart's personal religion that we suddenly lose all enthusiasm. E8

———

We of the nervous West are victims of the philosophy of activism tragically misunderstood. Getting and spending, going and returning, organizing and promoting, buying and selling, working and playing — this alone constitutes living. If we are not making plans or working to carry out plans already made we feel that we are failures, that we are sterile, unfruitful eunuchs, parasites on the body of society. The gospel of work, as someone has called it, has crowded out the gospel of Christ in many Christian churches. G136

———

In an effort to get the work of the Lord done we often lose contact with the Lord of the work and quite literally wear our people out as well. I have heard more than one pastor boast that his church was a "live" one, pointing to the printed calendar as proof — something on every night and several meetings during the day. Of course this proves nothing except that the pastor and the church are being guided by a bad spiritual philosophy. A great many of these time-consuming activities are useless and others plain ridiculous. "But," say the eager beavers who run the religious squirrel cages, "they provide fellowship and they hold our people together." G136

——

... many, perhaps most, of the activities engaged in by the average church do not contribute in any way to the accomplishing of the true work of Christ on earth. G137

——

Work that is only religious work and religious activity can be done by ungifted men and women and it can be done within the framework of the Christian church. But it will wind up with the judgment upon it that it is only a product of a human mind. K39

Afterlife

Personally I find it difficult to picture the resurrection and the future life. G69

——

I have pored over the Book of Revelation without receiving much help in my attempt to visualize the life to come. G69

——

I believe with unshakable confidence that our Lord has gone to prepare us a place and that He will come to take us unto Himself, but I cannot form a mental image of it. G69

——

At the close of every obituary of His believing children, God adds the word *henceforth*! After every biography, God adds the word *henceforth*! There will be a tomorrow and this is a reason for Christian joy. J85

Belief and Unbelief

Since believing is looking, it can be done without special equipment or religious paraphernalia. God has seen to it that the one life-and-death essential can never be subject to the caprice of accident. Equipment can break down or get lost, water can leak away, records can be destroyed by fire, the minister can be delayed or the church burn down. All these are external to the soul and are subject to accident or mechanical failure: but *looking* is of the heart and can be done successfully by any man standing up or kneeling down or lying in his last agony a thousand miles from any church.

Since believing is looking it can be done *any time*. No season is superior to another season for this sweetest of all acts. A94

———

The temptation to make our relation to God judicial instead of personal is very strong. Believing for salvation has these days been reduced to a once-done act that requires no further attention. C11

———

In our constant struggle to believe we are likely to overlook the simple fact that a bit of healthy disbelief is sometimes as needful as faith to the welfare of our souls. C119

———

I have met Christians with no more discrimination than the ostrich. Because they must believe certain things, they feel that they must believe everything. Because they are called upon to accept the invisible they go right on to accept the incredible. God can and does work miracles; ergo, everything that passes for a miracle must be of God. [C120]

———

In our eagerness to make converts we allow our hearers to absorb the idea that they can deal with their entire responsibility once and for all by an act of believing. This is in some vague way supposed to honor grace and glorify God, whereas actually it is to make Christ the author of a grotesque, unworkable system that has no counterpart in the Scriptures of truth. [D16]

———

If we only believe hard enough we'll make it somehow. So goes the popular chant. What you believe is not important. Only believe. Jew, Catholic, nature mystic, deist, occultist, swami, Mormon, Sufi, moon-struck poet without religious convictions, political dreamer or aspirant for a cottage on Uranus or Mars—just keep on believing, and peace, it will be wonderful. Soon a disease-free, warless world will emerge from the mists inhabited by a colorless, creedless, classless race where men will brothers be for a' that and a' that. [E54]

———

True faith requires that we believe everything God has said about Himself, but also that we believe everything He has said about us. Until we believe that we are as bad as God says we are, we can never believe that He will do for us what He says He will do. [E56]

———

Every man will have to decide for himself whether or not he can afford the terrible luxury of unbelief. [G118]

Bible

... new world will arise out of the religious mists when we approach our Bible with the idea that it is not only a book which was once spoken, but a book which is now speaking. A82

If you would follow on to know the Lord, come at once to the open Bible expecting it to speak to you. Do not come with the notion that it is a *thing* which you may push around at your convenience. A82

The Spirit-filled walk demands, for instance, that we live in the Word of God as a fish lives in the sea. By this I do not mean that we study the Bible merely, nor that we take a "course" in Bible doctrine. I mean that we should "meditate day and night" in the sacred Word, that we should love it and feast upon it and digest it every hour of the day and night. B125

The most realistic book in the world is the Bible. God is real, men are real and so is sin and so are death and hell, toward which sin inevitably leads. D93

There is scarcely anything so dull and meaningless as Bible doctrine taught for its own sake. Truth divorced from life is not truth in its Biblical sense, but something else and something less. E25

The Bible is among other things a book of revealed truth.

That is, certain facts are revealed that could not be discovered by the most brilliant mind. These facts are of such a nature as to be past finding out. E25

———

The Bible . . . is more than a volume of hitherto unknown facts about God, man and the universe. It is a book of exhortation based upon those facts. By far the greater portion of the book is devoted to an urgent effort to persuade people to alter their ways and bring their lives into harmony with the will of God as set forth in its pages. E27

———

. . . the Holy Scriptures tell us what we could never learn any other way: They tell us what we are, who we are, how we got here, why we are here and what we are required to do while we remain here. E30

———

In bringing many sons unto glory God works with whatever He has in whatever way He can and by whatever means He can, respecting always His own gift to us, the freedom of our wills. But of all means He uses the Bible is the best. E67

———

The Word of God well understood and religiously obeyed is the shortest route to spiritual perfection. E67

———

. . . the Bible, to be understood by its readers, must condescend to tell of eternal things in the language of time. G89

———

. . . we find the Bible difficult because we try to read it

as we would read any other book, and it is not the same as any other book. [H26]

———

Some believe and some do not; some are morally receptive and some are not; some have spiritual capacity and some have not. It is to those who do and are and have that the Bible is addressed. Those who do not and are not and have not will read it in vain. [H27]

———

The Bible is a supernatural book and can be understood only by supernatural aid. [H29]

———

Seen one way, the Bible is a book of doom. [H112]

———

After the Bible the next most valuable book for the Christian is a *good* hymnal. [H150]

———

There isn't anything dated in the Book of God. When I go to my Bible, I find dates but no dating. I mean that I find the sense and the feeling that everything here belongs to me. [131]

———

You will not find a single book of the Bible that does not have godly exhortation. There is not a single Bible portion that God wants us to study just to get a cranium full of knowledge or learning.

The Bible always presents the truth and then makes the application: "Now, if this is true, you ought to do something about it!" That is the meaning of moral application of spiritual truth. [1121]

———

I cannot think of even one lonely passage in the New Testament which speaks of Christ's revelation, manifestation, appearing or coming that is not directly linked with moral conduct, faith and spiritual holiness. [1145]

———

The Word of God is the foundation of our peace and rest. [174]

———

... get alone with God and His Word every day. I recommend that you turn off the radio and the television and let your soul delight in the fellowship and the mercies of God. [174]

———

... you can be perfectly free to go to your Bible with assurance that you will find Jesus Christ everywhere in its pages. [1155]

———

Let us read the Bible as the Word of God and never apologize for finding Jesus Christ throughout its pages, for Jesus Christ is what the Bible is all about! [1156]

Body, Soul and Spirit

Confirmation, baptism, holy communion, confession of faith: none of these nor all of them together can turn flesh into spirit nor make of a son of Adam a son of God. [B111]

———

... it is proper to say that man is made for the earth, it is actually necessary to say that man's body is made for the earth. It was his body that was taken from the dust of the ground, for man became a living soul when God breathed into his nostrils the breath of life. The image of God was not in the body of the man, but in the spirit that made him man. The body is simply the instrument through which the soul manifests itself down here—that is all. [J109]

———

We should not think it is humility to berate and cry down this body which God has given us. It serves us well, but it has no power in itself. It has no will of its own. The body cannot express affection or emotion. [J109]

———

The human body has no thought processes. Our human thought processes lie within the soul, in the human mind, in the human spirit. But God has ordained that it is through the instrument of the body that our ability to think shines forth and expresses itself. [J110]

———

There is nothing evil in matter itself. Evil lies in the spirit. Evils of the heart, of the mind, of the soul, of the spirit—these have to do with man's sin, and the only reason the human body does evil is because the human spirit uses it to do evil. [J110]

———

In the time of our departure, the body that He gave us will disintegrate and drop away like a cocoon, for the spirit of the man soars away to the presence of God. [J115]

Books

The worst thing a book can do for a Christian is to leave him with the impression that he has received from it anything really good; the best it can do is to point the way to the Good he is seeking. The function of a good book is to stand like a signpost directing the reader toward the Truth and the Life. [B15]

———

The work of a good book is to incite the reader to moral action, to turn his eyes toward God and urge him forward. [B15]

———

To think without a proper amount of good reading is to limit our thinking to our own tiny plot of ground. The crop cannot be large. To observe only and neglect reading is to deny ourselves the immense value of other people's observations; and since the better books are written by trained observers the loss is sure to be enormous. Extensive reading without the discipline of practical observation will lead to bookishness and artificiality. Reading and observing without a great deal of meditating will fill the mind with learned lumber that will always remain alien to us. Knowledge to be our own must be digested by thinking. [H147]

———

The best book is not one that informs merely, but one that stirs the reader up to inform himself. The best writer is one that goes with us through the world of ideas like a friendly guide who walks beside us through the forest pointing out to us a hundred natural wonders we had not noticed before. So we learn from him to see for ourselves and soon we have no need for our guide. [H149]

Brotherhood

It is ironic that this generation which more than any other in history preaches the brotherhood of man is also the generation most torn by unbrotherly strife. [D108]

———

Always it is more important that we retain a right spirit toward others than that we bring them to our way of thinking, even if our way is right. [E92]

———

. . . God has made us for each other, and it is His will and desire that Christian believers should understand and appreciate one another. [J165]

Change

Only the unchanged and the unchanging should be accounted worthy of lasting consideration by beings made in the image of God. [D89]

———

Every human being is in a state of becoming, of passing from what he was to what he is to be. [D127]

———

Plain horse sense ought to tell us that anything that makes no change in the man who professes it makes no difference to God either, and it is an easily observable fact that for countless numbers of persons the change from no-faith to faith makes no actual difference in the life. [H31]

———

The newborn Christian is a migrant; he has come into the kingdom of God from his old home in the kingdom of man and he must get set for the violent changes that will inevitably follow. [H62]

Children

Most of us are acquainted with churches that teach the Bible to their children from their tenderest years, give them long instruction in the catechism, drill them further in pastor's classes, and still never produce in them a living Christianity nor a virile godliness. Their members show no evidence of having passed from death unto life. [C35]

———

The desire to appear broad-minded is one not easy to overcome, for it is rooted in our ego and is simply a none-too-subtle form of pride. In the name of broad-mindedness many a Christian home has been opened to literature that sprang not from a broad mind, but from a mind little and dirty and polluted with evil.

We require our children to wipe their feet before entering the house. Dare we demand less of the literature that comes into our home? [E79]

Choice

God has indeed lent to every man the power to lock his heart and stalk away darkly into his self-chosen night,

16

as He has lent to every man the ability to respond to
His overtures of grace, but while the "no" choice may
be ours, the "yes" choice is always God's. [B49]

———

"If any man will," said our Lord, and thus freed every
man and placed the Christian life in the realm of
voluntary choice. [E38]

———

If a man *chooses* the will of God he is not denying but
exercising his right of choice. [G31]

———

The choices of life, not the compulsions, reveal character. [H158]

Christ

To many Christians Christ is little more than an idea,
or at best an ideal; He is not a fact. [C49]

———

The meek and lowly Jesus has displaced the high and
holy Jesus in the minds of millions. The vibrant note of
triumph is missing in our witness. A sad weeping Jesus
offers us His quiet sympathy in our griefs and
temptations, but He appears to be as helpless as we are
when the pressure is on. His pale feminine face looks at
us from the "holy picture" of the Catholic and the
Easter card of the Protestant. We give Him our sympathy,
but scarcely our confidence. The helpless Christ of the
crucifix and the vacuous-countenanced Christ that looks
out in sweet innocence from the walls of our evangelical

homes is all one and the same. The Catholics rescue Him by bringing a Queen of Heaven to His aid. But we Protestants have no helper. So we sing pop choruses to cheer our drooping spirits and hold panel discussions in the plaintive hope that someone will come up with the answer to our scarce-spoken complaint. [C72]

———

Our great honor lies in being just what Jesus was and is. To be accepted by those who accept Him, rejected by all who reject Him, loved by those who love Him and hated by everyone that hates Him. What greater glory could come to any man? [D59]

———

The flush and excitement of the soul in love must be sought in the New Testament or in the biographies of the saints; we look for them in vain among the professed followers of Christ in our day.

Now if there is any reality within the whole sphere of human experience that is by its very nature worthy to challenge the mind, charm the heart and bring the total life to a burning focus, it is the reality that revolves around the Person of Christ. [E8]

———

The Christ of popular Christianity has a weak smile and a halo. He has become Someone-up-There who likes people, at least some people, and these are grateful but not too impressed. If they need Him, He also needs them. [F43]

———

While Christ was the perfect example of the healthy normal man, He yet did not live a normal life. He sacrificed many pure enjoyments to give Himself to the holy work of moral rescue. His conduct was determined not by what was legitimate or innocent, but by our human need. He pleased not Himself but lived for the emergency; and as He was so are we in this world. G104

———

Christ is not one of many ways to approach God, nor is He the best of several ways; He is the only way. *"I am the way, the truth, and the life: no man cometh unto the Father, but by me."* To believe otherwise is to be something less than a Christian. G135

———

To be called to follow Christ is a high honor; higher indeed than any honor men can bestow upon each other. H11

———

Jesus Christ is a Man come to save men. H12

———

My criticism of most of our Bible conferences is that we spend our time counting again the treasures that we have in Christ but we never arrive at the place where any of that which is in Christ gets into us. H105

———

Salvation comes not by "accepting the finished work" or "deciding for Christ." It comes by believing on the Lord Jesus Christ, the whole, living, victorious Lord who, as God and man, fought our fight and won it, accepted our debt as His own and paid it, took our sins and died under them and rose again to set us free. This is the true Christ, and nothing less will do.

But something less is among us, nevertheless, and we do well to identify it so that we may repudiate it. That something is a poetic fiction, a product of the romantic imagination and maudlin religious fancy. It is a Jesus, gentle, dreamy, shy, sweet, almost effeminate, and marvelously adaptable to whatever society He may find Himself in. He is cooed over by women disappointed in love, patronized by pro tem celebrities and recommended by psychiatrists as a model of a well-integrated personality. He is used as a means to almost any carnal end, but He is never acknowledged as Lord. These quasi Christians follow a quasi Christ. They want His help but not His interference. They will flatter Him but never obey Him. [H142]

———

Christ has been explained, humanized, demoted. Many professed Christians no longer expect Him to usher in a new order, they are not at all sure that He is able to do so; or if He does, it will be with the help of art, education, science and technology; that is, with the help of man. This revised expectation amounts to disillusionment for many. And of course no one can become too radiantly happy over a King of kings who has been stripped of His crown or a Lord of lords who has lost His sovereignty. [H155]

———

I believe that Jesus meant to shake us up! [J70]

———

I delight in the inward knowledge that Jesus Christ, the Son of God and our coming Lord, will be sufficient for every situation which is yet to come to pass. We will never panic along with this present world system as long as we are fortified with our knowledge of who Jesus Christ really is. J74

———

This is, in essence, the charge that John levels at human kind: Jesus Christ, the Word of God, was in the world, and the world failed to recognize Him. J89

———

Our great need, then, is simply Jesus Christ. He is what we need. He has what we need. He knows what we need to know. He has the ability to do in us what we cannot do—working in us that which is well-pleasing in God's sight. J129

———

God's revelation says that Jesus Christ is the eternal Victor, triumphant over sin and death! That is why He is the Head of the new creation which has upon it the banner of perfectivity rather than temporality and the mark of life forevermore rather than the mark of death. K150

"Accepting" Christ

P, 7 6 Everything is made to center upon the initial act of "accepting" Christ (a term, incidentally, which is not found in the Bible) and we are not expected thereafter to crave any further revelation of God to our souls. A16

———

We must assure our hearers that Christianity is now a proper and respectable thing and that Christ has become quite popular with political bigwigs, well-to-do business tycoons and the Hollywood swimming pool set. Thus assured, hell-deserving sinners are coming in droves to "accept" Christ for what they can get out of Him; and though one now and again may drop a tear as proof of his sincerity, it is hard to escape the conclusion that most of them are stooping to patronize the Lord of glory much as a young couple might fawn on a boresome but rich old uncle in order to be mentioned in his will later on. [D17]

———

... the formula "Accept Christ" has become a panacea of universal application, and I believe it has been fatal to many. [G18]

———

The trouble is that the whole "Accept Christ" attitude is likely to be wrong. It shows Christ applying to us rather than us to Him. It makes Him stand hat-in-hand awaiting our verdict on Him, instead of our kneeling with troubled hearts awaiting His verdict on us. It may even permit us to accept Christ by an impulse of mind or emotions, painlessly, at no loss to our ego and no inconvenience to our usual way of life. [G18]

———

To accept Christ is to form an attachment to the Person of our Lord Jesus altogether unique in human experience. The attachment is intellectual, volitional and emotional. [G18]

———

To accept Christ is to know the meaning of the words *"as he is, so are we in this world."* We accept His friends as our friends, His enemies as our enemies, His ways as our ways, His rejection as our rejection, His cross as our cross, His life as our life and His future as our future.

If this is what we mean when we advise the seeker to accept Christ we had better explain it to him. He may get into deep spiritual trouble unless we do. G19

———

To accept Christ it is necessary that we reject whatever is contrary to Him. This is a fact often overlooked by eager evangelists bent on getting results. G74

———

We are telling people that the easiest thing in the world is to *accept* Jesus Christ, and I wonder what has happened to our Christian theology which no longer contains any hint of what it should mean to be completely and utterly abandoned to Jesus Christ, our Lord and Saviour. J53

Second Advent of Christ

If the tender yearning is gone from the advent hope today there must be a reason for it; and I think I know what it is, or what they are, for there are a number of them. One is simply that popular fundamentalist theology has emphasized the utility of the cross rather than the beauty of the One who died on it. The saved man's relation to Christ has been made contractual instead of personal. The "work" of Christ has been stressed until it has eclipsed the person of Christ. Substitution has been allowed to supersede identification. What He did for me seems to be more important than what He is to me. Redemption is seen as an across-the-counter transaction which we "accept," and the whole thing lacks emotional content. We must love someone very much to stay awake and long for his coming, and that may explain the absence of power in the advent hope even among those who still believe in it. [D133]

————

It should be noted that there is a vast difference between the doctrine of Christ's coming and the *hope* of His coming. The first we may hold without feeling a trace of the second. Indeed there are multitudes of Christians today who hold the doctrine of the second coming. What I have talked about here is that overwhelming sense of anticipation that lifts the life onto a new plane and fills the heart with rapturous optimism. This is what we today lack. [H157]

————

Possibly nothing short of a world catastrophe that will destroy every false trust and turn our eyes once more upon the Man Christ Jesus will bring back the glorious hope to a generation that has lost it. [H157]

Teaching of Christ

The message of Christ lays hold upon a man with the intention to alter him, to mold him again after another image and make of him something altogether different from what he had been before. [C57]

————

The teachings of Christ reveal Him to be a realist in the finest meaning of that word. Nowhere in the Gospels do we find anything visionary or overoptimistic. He told His hearers the whole truth and let them make up their minds. He might grieve over the retreating form of an inquirer who could not face up to the truth, but He

never ran after him to try to win him with rosy promises.
He would have men follow Him, knowing the cost, or
He would let them go their ways. G116

———

What has Christ to offer to us that is sound, genuine
and desirable? He offers forgiveness of sins, inward
cleansing, peace with God, eternal life, the gift of the
Holy Spirit, victory over temptation, resurrection from
the dead, a glorified body, immortality and a dwelling
place in the house of the Lord forever. These are a few
benefits that come to us as a result of faith in Christ
and total committal to Him. Add to these the expanding
wonders and increasing glories that shall be ours through
the long, long reaches of eternity, and we get an imperfect
idea of what Paul called "the unsearchable riches of
Christ." G117

Christian

The true Christian ideal is not to be happy but to be
holy. B100

———

There is an evil which I have seen under the sun and
which in its effect upon the Christian religion may be
more destructive than Communism, Romanism and
Liberalism combined. It is the glaring disparity between
theology and practice among professing Christians. C51

———

One of the most stinging criticisms made against
Christians is that their minds are narrow and their hearts
small. C113

Christians have often been accused of being reactionary because they cannot get up any enthusiasm over the latest scheme that someone thinks up to bring in the millennium. [C156]

———

A real Christian is an odd number anyway. He feels supreme love for One whom he has never seen, talks familiarly every day to Someone he cannot see, expects to go to heaven on the virtue of Another, empties himself in order to be full, admits he is wrong so he can be declared right, goes down in order to get up, is strongest when he is weakest, richest when he is poorest, and happiest when he feels worst. He dies so he can live, forsakes in order to have, gives away so he can keep, sees the invisible, hears the inaudible, and knows that which passeth knowledge. [C156]

———

The average Christian is so cold and so contented with His wretched condition that there is no vacuum of desire into which the blessed Spirit can rush in satisfying fullness. [D7]

———

Those first believers turned to Christ with the full understanding that they were espousing an unpopular cause that could cost them everything. They knew they would henceforth be members of a hated minority group with life and liberty always in jeopardy. [D18]

———

The most godly Christian is the one who knows himself best, and no one who knows himself will believe that he deserves anything better than hell.

The man who knows himself least is likely to have a cheerful if groundless confidence in his own moral worth. Such a man has less trouble believing that he will inherit an eternity of bliss because his concepts are only quasi-Christian, being influenced strongly by chimney-corner scripture and old wives' tales. He thinks of heaven as being very much like California without the heat and smog, and himself as inhabiting a splendiferous palace with all modern conveniences, and wearing a heavily bejeweled crown. Throw in a few angels and you have the vulgar picture of the future life held by the devotees of popular Christianity.

This is the heaven that appears in the saccharin ballads of the guitar-twanging rockabilly gospellers that clutter up the religious scene today. That the whole thing is completely unrealistic and contrary to the laws of the moral universe seems to make no difference to anyone. D36

———

. . . we are never sure where a true Christian may be found. One thing we do know: the more like Christ he is the less likely it will be that a newspaper reporter will be seeking him out. D55

———

It might be well for us Christians to listen less to the news commentaries and more to the voice of the Spirit. E36

———

Here's how the file card works when it gets into the Christian life and begins to create mental habits: It divides the Bible into sections fitted to the days of the year, and compels the Christian to read according to rule. No matter what the Holy Spirit may be trying to say to a man, still he goes on reading where the card tells him, dutifully checking it off each day.

Every Spirit-led saint knows that there are times when he is held by an inward pressure to one chapter, or even one verse, for days at a time while he wrestles with God till some truth does its work within him. To leave that present passage to follow a pre-arranged reading schedule is for him wholly impossible. He is in the land of the free Spirit, and reality is appearing before him to break and humble and lift and liberate and cheer. But only the free soul can know the glory of this. To this the heart bound by system will be forever a stranger. [E71]

———

Our Christian testimony has created a certain expectation in the minds of our friends, and rather than jeopardize our standing with them we dutifully act in accordance with their expectations even though we have no personal conviction about the matter. We are simply afraid not to do what people expect of us. We cannot face our public after we have failed to do what we know they expected us to do. [E98]

———

A free Christian should act from within with a total disregard for the opinions of others. If a course is right he should take it because it is right, not because he is afraid not to take it. And if it is wrong he should avoid it though he lose every earthly treasure and even his very life as a consequence. [E98]

———

We Christians must simplify out lives or lose untold treasures on earth and in eternity. [A103]

We of the Christian faith need not go onto the defensive. The man of the world is the dreamer, not the Christian. The sinner can never be quite himself. All his life he must pretend. He must act as if he were never going to die, and yet he knows too well that he is. He must act as if he had not sinned, when in his deep heart he knows very well that he has. [E108]

———

Many Christians never get beyond Bethel. God is in their thoughts, but He is not first. [E109]

———

Surely the days are evil and the times are waxing late, but the true Christian is not caught unawares. He has been forewarned of just such times as these and has been expecting them. [E131]

———

The Christian believes that in Christ he has died, yet he is more alive than before and he fully expects to live forever. [G11]

———

The Christian soon learns that if he would be victorious as a son of heaven among men on earth he must not follow the common pattern of mankind, but rather the contrary. That he may be safe he puts himself in jeopardy; he loses his life to save it and is in danger of losing it if he attempts to preserve it. He goes down to get up. If he refuses to go down he is already down, but when he starts down he is on his way up.

He is strongest when he is weakest and weakest when he is strong. Though poor he has the power to make others rich, but when he becomes rich his ability to enrich others vanishes. He has most after he has given most away and has least when he possesses most.

He may be and often is highest when he feels lowest and most sinless when he is most conscious of sin. He is wisest when he knows that he knows not and knows least when he has acquired the greatest amount of knowledge. He sometimes does most by doing nothing and goes furthest when standing still. . .

He loves supremely One whom he has never seen, and though himself poor and lowly he talks familarly with One who is King of all kings and Lord of all lords, and is aware of no incongruity in so doing. G12

There are many other happy exchanges we Christians may make if we will, among them being our ignorance for His knowledge, our folly for His wisdom, our demerit for His merit, and our sad morality for His blessed immortality and faith for sight at last. G34

What the Christian used to be is altogether the least important thing about him. What he is yet to be is all that should concern him. G45

The ideal to which the Christian aspires is not to walk in the perfect way but to be transformed by the renewing of his mind and conformed to the likeness of Christ. G54

The average Christian these days is a harmless enough thing. God knows. He is a child wearing with considerable

30

self-consciousness the harness of the warrior; he is a sick eaglet that can never mount up with wings; he is a spent pilgrim who has given up the journey and sits with a waxy smile trying to get what pleasure he can from sniffing the wilted flowers he has plucked by the way. G72

———

The quest of the modern Christian is likely to be for peace of mind and spiritual joy, with a good degree of material prosperity thrown in as an external proof of the divine favor. G124

———

Christians have fallen into the habit of accepting the noisiest and most notorious among them as the best and the greatest. They too have learned to equate popularity with excellence, and in open defiance of the Sermon on the Mount they have given their approval not to the meek but to the self-assertive; not to the mourner but to the self-assured; not to the pure in heart who see God but to the publicity hunter who seeks headlines. H96

———

Those Christians who belong to the evangelical wing of the church (which I firmly believe is the only one that even approximates New Testament Christianity) have over the last-half century shown an increasing impatience with things invisible and eternal and have demanded and got a host of things visible and temporal to satisfy their fleshly appetites. Without Biblical authority, or any other right under the sun, carnal religious leaders have introduced a host of attractions that serve no purpose except to provide entertainment for the retarded saints. [H136]

———

Christians now chatter learnedly about things simple believers have always taken for granted. They are on the defensive, trying to prove things that a previous generation never doubted. We have allowed unbelievers to get us in a corner and have given them the advantage by permitting them to choose the time and place of encounter. We smart under the attack of the quasi-Christian unbeliever, and the nervous, self-conscious defense we make is called "the religious dialogue."

Under the scornful attack of the religious critic real Christians who ought to know better are now "rethinking" their faith. Scarcely anything has escaped the analysts. With a Freudian microscope they examine everything: foreign missions, the Book of Genesis, the inspiration of the Scriptures, morals, all tried and proven methods, polygamy, liquor, sex, prayer—all have come in for inquisition by those who engage in the contemporary dialogue. Adoration has given way to celebration in the holy place, if indeed any holy place remains to this generation of confused Christians.

The causes of the decline of apocalyptic expectation are many, not the least being the affluent society in which we live. If the rich man with difficulty enters the kingdom of God, then it would be logical to conclude that a society having the highest percentage of well-to-do persons in it would have the lowest percentage of Christians, all things else being equal. If the "deceitfulness of riches" chokes the Word and makes it unfruitful, then this would be the day of near-fruitless preaching, at least in the opulent West. And if surfeiting and drunkenness and worldly cares tend to unfit the Christian for the coming of Christ, then this generation of Christians should be the least prepared for that event. H153

———

One of the biggest problems of even the most ardent Christian these days is to find a parking place for the shiny chariot that transports him effortlessly to the house of God where he hopes to prepare his soul for the world to come. H154

———

The popular image of the man of God as a smiling, congenial, asexual religious mascot whose handshake is always soft and whose head is always bobbing in the perpetual Yes of universal acquiescence is not the image found in the Scriptures of truth. H167

———

. . . we are still living in a wicked and adulterous generation and I must confess that the Christians I meet who really amount to something for the Saviour are very much out of key and out of tune with their generation. I41

———

. . . . the Christian's future is still before him. I will give you time to smile at that, because it sounds like a self-evident bromide if ever one was uttered. But I assure you that it is not a self-evident banality; it is rather a proof that we ought to ponder soberly the fact that many Christians already have their future behind them. Their glory is behind them. The only future they have is their past. They are always lingering around the cold ashes of yesterday's burned-out campfire. Their testimonies indicate it, their outlook and their uplook reveal it and their downcast look betrays it! Above all, their backward look indicates it. I always get an uneasy feeling when I find myself with people who have nothing to discuss but the glories of the days that are past. [180]

The Christian is dead and yet he lives forever. He died to himself and yet he lives in Christ.

The reason he lives is because of the death of another.

The Christian saves his own life by losing it and he is in danger of losing it by trying to save it.

It is an interesting thing that when he wants to get up, the Christian always starts down, for God's way up is always down, even though that is contrary to common sense. It is also contrary to the finest wisdom on the earth, because the foolish things of God are wiser than anything on this earth. [1139]

People in the Christian churches who put their own convenience and their own comfort and their own selfish interests ahead of the claims of the gospel of Jesus Christ surely need to get down on their knees with an open Bible—and if they are honest as they search their own hearts, they will be shocked at what they find! [J72]

I am sure that our Lord is looking for heavenly-minded Christians. His Word encourages us to trust Him with such a singleness of purpose that He is able to deliver us from the fear of death and the uncertainties of tomorrow. [J116]

The believing Christian who sees in the creation of all things the setting forth of the wonder and glory of Jesus

Christ as Lord and Sovereign will have no more unholy
days. He will no longer be inclined to divide existence
between secular interests and holy interests. There is a
divine sanctification of everything in his life when the
believer fully realizes that God has made His creation
as a garment to show forth the Lord Jesus Christ. [J158]

Christianity

Christianity takes for granted the absence of any self-
help and offers a power which is nothing less than the
power of God. [B88]

___

Values which Christ has declared to be false are brought
back into evangelical favor and promoted as the very
life and substance of the Christian way. How eagerly do
we seek the approval of this or that man of worldly
reputation. How shamefully do we exploit the converted
celebrity. [B88]

___

Deity indwelling men! That, I say, is Christianity, and
no man has experienced rightly the power of Christian
belief until he has known this for himself as a living
reality. Everything else is preliminary to this. [E98]

___

Many of us Christians have become extremely skillful
in arranging our lives so as to admit the truth of
Christianity without being embarrassed by its
implications. We arrange things so that we can get on
well enough without divine aid, while at the same time

ostensibly seeking it. We boast in the Lord but watch carefully that we never get caught depending on Him. [C49]

———

... the whole evangelical world is to a large extent unfavorable to healthy Christianity. And I am not thinking of Modernism either. I mean rather the Bible-believing crowd that bears the name of orthodoxy.

We may as well face it: the whole level of spirituality among us is low. We have measured ourselves by ourselves until the incentive to seek higher plateaus in the things of the Spirit is all but gone. Large and influential sections of the world of fundamental Christianity have gone overboard for practices wholly unscriptural, altogether unjustifiable in the light of historic Christian truth and deeply damaging to the inner life of the individual Christian. They have imitated the world, sought popular favor, manufactured delights to substitute for the joy of the Lord and produced a cheap and synthetic power to substitute for the power of the Holy Ghost. [E12]

———

Evangelical Christianity is now tragically below the New Testament standard. Worldliness is an accepted part of our way of life. Our religious mood is social instead of spiritual. We have lost the art of worship. We are not producing saints. Our models are successful businessmen, celebrated athletes and theatrical personalities. We carry on our religious activities after the methods of the modern advertiser. Our homes have been turned into theaters. Our literature is shallow and our hymnody borders on sacrilege. And scarcely anyone appears to care. [E36]

By "instant Christianity" I mean the kind found almost everywhere in gospel circles and which is born of the notion that we may discharge our total obligation to our own souls by one act of faith, or at most by two, and be relieved thereafter of all anxiety about our spiritual condition. [G23]

———

Instead Christianity tends to make the faith act terminal and so smothers the desire for spiritual advance. It fails to understand the true nature of the Christian life, which is not static but dynamic and expanding. It overlooks the fact that a new Christian is a living organism as certainly as a new baby is, and must have nourishment and exercise to assure normal growth. It does not consider that the act of faith in Christ sets up a personal relationship between two intelligent moral beings, God and the reconciled man, and no single encounter between God and a creature made in His image could ever be sufficient to establish an intimate friendship between them. [G24]

———

The notion that we enter the Christian life by an act of acceptance is true, but that is not all the truth. There is much more to it than that. Christianity involves an acceptance and a repudiation, an affirmation and a denial. And this not only at the moment of conversion but continually thereafter day by day in all the battle of life till the great conflict is over and the Christian is home from the wars. [G74]

———

Let us not be shocked by the suggestion that there are disadvantages to the life in Christ. There most certainly

are. Abel was murdered, Joseph was sold into slavery,
Daniel was thrown into the den of lions, Stephen was
stoned to death, Paul was beheaded, and a noble army
of martyrs was put to death by various painful methods
all down the long centuries. And where the hostility
did not lead to such violence (and mostly it did not and
does not) the sons of this world nevertheless managed
to make it tough for the children of God in a thousand
cruel ways. G74

———

. . . large numbers of supposedly sound Christian believers
know nothing at all about personal communion with
God; and there lies one of the greatest weaknesses of
present-day Christianity. G83

———

Christianity today is man-centered, not God-centered.
God is made to wait patiently, even respectfully, on the
whims of men. The image of God currently popular is
that of a distracted Father, struggling in heartbroken
desperation to get people to accept a Saviour of whom
they feel no need and in whom they have very little
interest. To persuade these self-sufficient souls to respond
to His generous offers God will do almost anything,
even using salesmanship methods and talking down to
them in the chummiest way imaginable. This view of
things is, of course, a kind of religious romanticism
which, while it often uses flattering and sometimes
embarrassing terms in praise of God, manages
nevertheless to make man the star of the show. H27

———

. . . popular Christianity has as one of its most effective
talking points the idea that God exists to help people
to get ahead in this world. H57

Christless Christianity sounds contradictory but it exists as a real phenomenon in our day. [H124]

———

Any objection to the carryings on of our present golden-calf Christianity is met with the triumphant reply, "But we are winning them!" And winning them to what? To true discipleship? To cross-carrying? To self-denial? To separation from the world? To crucifixion of the flesh? To holy living? To nobility of character? To a despising of the world's treasures? To hard self-discipline? To love for God? To total committal to Christ? Of course the answer to all these questions is *no.* [H136]

———

There is a notion abroad that Christianity is on its last legs, or possibly already dead and just too weak to lie down. [H137]

———

There is a purging element in Christianity. [J42]

———

Christianity to the average evangelical church member is simply an avenue to a good and pleasant time, with a little biblical devotional material thrown in for good measure! [J72]

———

Contrary to the opinion held by many would-be religious leaders in the world, Christianity was never intended to be an "ethical system" with Jesus Christ at the head.

Our Lord did not come into the world 2,000 years ago to launch Christianity as a new religion or a new system. He came into this world with eternal purpose. He came as the center of all things. Actually, He came to be our religion, if you wish to put it that way.

He came in person, in the flesh, to be God's salvation to the very ends of the earth. He did not come just to delegate power to others to heal or cure or bless. He came to *be* the blessing, for all the blessings and the full glory of God are to be found in His person. [K71]

————

... all Christianity offers is Jesus Christ the Lord, and Him alone—for He is enough! Your relation to Jesus Christ is really the all-important matter in this life.

That is both good news and bad news. It is good news for all who have met our Saviour and know Him intimately and personally. It is bad news for those who hope to get into heaven some other way! [K73]

Church

The churches (even the gospel churches) are worldly in spirit, morally anemic, on the defensive, imitating instead of initiating and in a wretched state generally because for two full generations they have been told that justification is no more than a "not guilty" verdict pronounced by the Heavenly Father upon a sinner who can present the magic coin *faith* with the wondrous "open-sesame" engraved upon it. [B37]

————

The gradual disappearance of the idea and feeling of majesty from the Church is a sign and a portent. The revolt of the modern mind has had a heavy price, how heavy is becoming more apparent as the years go by. Our God has now become our servant to wait on our will. "The Lord is my *shepherd*," we say, instead of "*The Lord* is my shepherd," and the difference is as wide as the world. [B51]

———

Those overtones of religious delight which accompany truth when the Spirit illuminates it are all but missing from the Church today. [B81]

———

A church that is soundly rooted cannot be destroyed, but nothing can save a church whose root is dried up. No stimulation, no advertising campaigns, no gifts of money and no beautiful edifice can bring back life to the rootless tree. [C7]

———

Churches and Christian organizations have shown a tendency to fall into the same error that destroyed Israel: inability to receive admonition. [C28]

———

Don't defend your church or your organization against criticism. If the criticism is false it can do no harm. If it is true you need to hear it and do something about it. [C29]

———

In the Church of God two opposite dangers are to be recognized and avoided; they are a cold heart and a hot head. [C149]

Unquestionably there is not another institution in the world that talks as much and does as little as the church. Any factory that required as much raw material for so small a finished product would go bankrupt in six months. I have often thought that if one-tenth of one per cent of the prayers made in the churches of any ordinary American village on one Sunday were answered the country would be transformed overnight. [D34]

———

. . . the professed church seems to have learned nothing. We are still seeing as men see and judging after the manner of man's judgment. How much eager-beaver religious work is done out of a carnal desire to make good. How many hours of prayer are wasted beseeching God to bless projects that are geared to the glorification of little men. How much sacred money is poured out upon men who, in spite of their tear-in-the-voice appeals, nevertheless seek only to make a fair show in the flesh. [D58]

The Church is dedicated to things that matter. Quality matters. Let's not be led astray by the size of things. [D75]

———

Much that the church—even the evangelical church—is doing these days she is doing because she is afraid not to. [E15]

———

The true church has never sounded out public expectations before launching her crusades. Her leaders heard from God and went ahead wholly independent

of popular support or the lack of it. They knew their
Lord's will and did it, and their people followed them—
sometimes to triumph, oftener to insults and public
persecution—and their sufficient reward was the
satisfaction of being right in a wrong world. [E15]

———

The task of the church is twofold: to spread Christianity
throughout the world and to make sure that the
Christianity she spreads is the pure New Testament
kind. [E34]

———

The popular notion that the first obligation of the church
is to spread the gospel to the uttermost parts of the
earth is false. *Her first obligation is to be spiritually
worthy to spread it.* [E35]

———

It is God's purpose to give us ample power to carry the
fight to the enemy instead of sitting passively by and
allowing the enemy to carry the fight to us. If anyone is
to go on the defensive it should never be the church. [E97]

———

Of all work done under the sun religious work should
be the most open to examination. There is positively no
place in the church for sleight of hand or double talk.
Everything done by the churches should be completely
above suspicion. The true church will have nothing
to hide. Her books will be available to anyone for
inspection at any time. Her officers will insist upon an
audit by someone from the outside. [E122]

We Christians are the Church and whatever we do is what the Church is doing. The matter, therefore, is for each of us a personal one. Any forward step in the Church must begin with the individual. [F121]

———

Our churches these days are filled (or one-quarter filled) with a soft breed of Christian that must be fed on a diet of harmless fun to keep them interested. About theology they know little. Scarcely any of them have read even one of the great Christian classics, but most of them are familiar with religious fiction and spinetingling films. [G76]

———

Always the Church has been tempted to think of God by the use of images and forms, and always when she has so done she has fallen into externalism and spiritual decay. [G90]

———

The center of attraction in a true church is the Lord Jesus Christ. [G136]

———

The world wants the church to add a dainty spiritual touch to its carnal schemes, and to be there to help it to its feet and put it to bed when it comes home drunk with fleshly pleasures.

In the first place the church has received no such commision from her Lord, and in the second place the world has never shown much disposition to listen to the church when she speaks in her true prophetic voice. [H139]

God fully expects the church of Jesus Christ to prove itself a miraculous group in the very midst of a hostile world. Christians of necessity must be in contact with the world but in being and spirit ought to be separated from the world—and as such, we should be the most amazing people in the world. [139]

___

... the Christian church seems to have a variety of concerns, but in reality it has only one reason for being—and that is to show forth the life and mercy and grace of Jesus Christ. [J150]

___

... when Jesus Christ by His Spirit meets with two of His believing people, you have a church! You have it without any upkeep and without any overhead and without any elections. But Jesus Christ must be central and His Presence must be known among His people. [J157]

___

... mortality and temporality are written all across the church of Christ in the world today because so many persons are trying to do with human genius and power of the flesh what only God can do through the Holy Spirit. [K39]

___

In the Body of Christ there are no insignificant congregations. [K48]

___

... there are no little churches; all churches are the same size in God's sight." [K48]

... we are a part of that great Christian body that goes back to Pentecost. I believe in a true kind of apostolic succession, not a succession of bishops and men with names and organizations, but a living organism vitally a part of the true church of Christ that began when the Holy Ghost came upon a body of believers and made them one, making them God's people in a way that none ever had been before! K61

———

Only the Christian church in the midst of all the world religions is able to proclaim the Bible's good news that God, the Creator and Redeemer, will bring a new order into being! K147

Civilization

Every age has its own characteristics. Right now we are in an age of religious complexity. The simplicity which is in Christ is rarely found among us. In its stead are programs, methods, organizations and a world of nervous activities which occupy time and attention. A17

———

... the most ominous sign of the coming destruction of our country is the passing of the American home. E105

———

... our Western civilization is on its way to perishing. It has many commendable qualities, most of which it has borrowed from the Christian ethic, but it lacks the element of moral wisdom that would give it permanence.

Future historians will record that we of the twentieth century had intelligence enough to create a great civilization but not the moral wisdom to preserve it. [H49]

———

Were men everywhere to ignore the things that matter little or not at all and give serious attention to the few really important things, most of the walls that divide men would be thrown down at once and a world of endless sufferings ended. [H116]

———

Why is it that the generation that is talking the most and making the most of unity is also the generation that has the greatest amount of hate and suspicion, the biggest bombs and the largest armies? [K113]

Complacency

One of the greatest foes of the Christian is religious complacency. [C55]

———

Religious complacency is encountered almost everywhere among Christians these days, and its presence is a sign and a prophecy. For every Christian will become at last what his desires have made him. We are all the sum total of our hungers. [C55]

———

It is a grave error for us evangelicals to assume that the children of God are all in our communion and that all who are not associated with us are *ipso facto* enemies of the Lord. The Pharisees made that mistake and crucified Christ as a consequence. [H19]

———

The complacency of Christians is the scandal of Christianity. [H38]

Conduct

Human nature tends to excesses by a kind of evil magnetic attraction. We instinctively run to one of two extremes, and that is why we are so often in error.

A proof of this propensity to extremes is seen in the attitude of the average Christian toward the devil. I have observed among spiritual persons a tendency either to ignore him altogether or to make too much of him. Both are wrong. [D40]

———

... most Christians would be better pleased if the Lord did not inquire into their personal affairs too closely. They want Him to save them, keep them happy and take them to heaven at last, but not to be too inquisitive about their conduct or service. [G105]

———

The Lord loves the artless, the candid, the childlike. He cannot work with those who argue or bargain or plead or excuse themselves. [G106]

———

Tie up the loose ends of your life. Begin to tithe; institute family prayer; pay up your debts as far as possible and make some kind of frank arrangement with every creditor you cannot pay immediately; make restitution as far as you can; set aside time to pray and search the Scriptures; surrender wholly to the will of God. You will be surprised and delighted with the results. [H40]

———

To do a wrong act a man must for the moment think wrong; he must exercise bad judgment. [H46]

———

It is only after we yield to Jesus Christ and begin to follow Him that we become concerned about the laxity and thoughtlessness of our daily lives. We begin to grieve about the way we have been living and we become convicted that there should continue to be aimlessness and futility and carelessness in our Christian walk. [I124]

———

In our Christian fellowship, we should be known for being perfectly frank and wholly honest, for honesty has a good root that will also produce other sterling Christian virtues. [J20]

———

There are so many things that are done in the world by Christians that are not really bad—they are just trivial. [K125]

Consecration

Every soul belongs to God and exists by His pleasure. God being Who and What He is, and we being who and what we are, the only thinkable relation between us is one of full lordship on His part and complete submission on ours. We owe Him every honor that it is in our power to give Him. Our everlasting grief lies in giving Him anything less. [A102]

———

The man who surrenders to Christ exchanges a cruel slave driver for a kind and gentle Master whose yoke is easy and whose burden is light. [A104]

———

The whole course of the life is upset by failure to put God where He belongs. [A107]

———

The whole man must make the decision before the heart can know any real satisfaction. God wants us all, and He will not rest till He gets us all. No part of the man will do. [A107]

———

By one act of consecration of our total selves to God we can make every subsequent act express that consecration. [A121]

———

... how can we live lives acceptable to God?

The answer is near thee, even in thy mouth. Vacate the throne room of your heart and enthrone Jesus there. Set Him in the focus of your heart's attention and stop wanting to be a hero. Make Him your all in all and try yourself to become less and less. Dedicate your entire life to His honor alone and shift the motives of your life from self to God. Let the reason back of your daily conduct be Christ and His glory, not yourself, not your

family nor your country nor your church. In all things
let Him have the preëminence. [D70]

Creation

Had there been no creation there could have been no
fall and no redemption. In the mind of God all things
occurred at once; but in the sequence of time creation
comes first. When Christ stepped down to take a body
and redeem fallen man He stepped into the framework
of an already existent nature. The very body that was
broken and the blood that was spilled were part of
creation, the product of the skilled fingers of God the
Father Almighty, maker of heaven and earth. [E119]

———

. . . creation is the setting forth of Jesus Christ as Lord
and Sovereign, for Jesus Christ is the purpose of God in
creation! [J158]

Cross

The cross is rough, and it is deadly, but it is effective. [A47]

———

The old cross slew men; the new cross entertains them.
The old cross condemned; the new cross amuses. The
old cross destroyed confidence in the flesh; the new
cross encourages it. The old cross brought tears and
blood; the new cross brings laughter. The flesh, smiling
and confident, preaches and sings about the cross; before
that cross it bows and toward that cross it points with
carefully staged histrionics—but upon that cross it will

not die, and the reproach of that cross it stubbornly refuses to bear. B59

———

... who but someone very old and very conservative would insist upon death as the appointed way to life? And who today is interested in a gloomy mysticism that would sentence its flesh to a cross and recommend self-effacing humility as a virtue actually to be practiced by modern Christians? B60

———

These are the arguments, along with many more flippant still, which are brought forward to give an appearance of wisdom to the hollow and meaningless cross of popular Christianity.

Doubtless there are many whose eyes are open to the tragedy of our times, but why are they so silent when their testimony is so sorely needed? In the name of Christ men have made void the cross of Christ. B61

———

Men have fashioned a golden cross with a graving tool, and before it they sit down to eat and drink and rise up to play. B61

———

Men crave life, but when they are told that life comes by the cross they cannot understand how it can be, for they have learned to associate with the cross such typical images as memorial placques, dim-lit aisles and ivy. So they reject the true message of the cross and with that message they reject the only hope of life known to the sons of men. B62

The life that halts short of the cross is but a fugitive and condemned thing, doomed at last to be lost beyond recovery. That life which goes to the cross and loses itself there to rise again with Christ is a divine and deathless treasure. Over it death hath no more dominion. Whoever refuses to bring his old life to the cross is but trying to cheat death, and no matter how hard he may struggle against it, he is nevertheless fated to lose his life at last. [B62]

———

The cross of Christ is the most revolutionary thing ever to appear among men. [C61]

———

The cross of old Roman times knew no compromise; it never made concessions. It won all its arguments by killing its opponent and silencing him for good. It spared not Christ, but slew Him the same as the rest. He was alive when they hung Him on that cross and completely dead when they took Him down six hours later. That was the cross the first time it appeared in Christian history. [C61]

———

The cross stands high above the opinions of men and to that cross all opinions must come at last for judgment. [C63]

———

We must do something about the cross, and one of two things only we can do—flee it or die upon it. [C63]

If we are wise we will do what Jesus did: endure the
cross and despise its shame for the joy that is set before
us. To do this is to submit the whole pattern of our
lives to be destroyed and built again in the power of an
endless life. And we shall find that it is more than
poetry, more than sweet hymnody and elevated feeling.
The cross will cut into our lives where it hurts worst,
sparing neither us nor our carefully cultivated
reputations. It will defeat us and bring our selfish lives
to an end. [C63]

In every Christian's heart there is a cross and a throne,
and the Christian is on the throne till he puts himself
on the cross; if he refuses the cross he remains on the
throne. Perhaps this is at the bottom of the backsliding
and worldliness among gospel believers today. We want
to be saved but we insist that Christ do all the dying.
No cross for us, no dethronement, no dying. We remain
king within the little kingdom of Mansoul and wear
our tinsel crown with all the pride of a Caesar; but we
doom ourselves to shadows and weakness and spiritual
sterility. [C66]

. . . the very power of the cross lies in the fact that it is
the wisdom of God and not the wisdom of man. [C79]

The cross would not be a cross to us if it destroyed in
us only the unreal and the artificial. It is when it goes
on to slay the best in us that its cruel sharpness is felt. [D53]

. . . it cannot be denied that the way of the cross is unpopular and that it brings a measure of reproach upon those who take it. [D53]

——

Christ calls men to carry a cross; we call them to have fun in His name. He calls them to forsake the world; we assure them that if they but accept Jesus the world is their oyster. He calls them to suffer; we call them to enjoy all the bourgeois comforts modern civilization affords. He calls them to self-abnegation and death; we call them to spread themselves like green bay trees or perchance even to become stars in a pitiful fifth-rate religious zodiac. He calls them to holiness; we call them to a cheap and tawdry happiness that would have been rejected with scorn by the least of the Stoic philosophers. [D141]

——

The man with a cross no longer controls his destiny; he lost control when he picked up his cross. That cross immediately became to him an all-absorbing interest, an overwhelming interference. No matter what he may desire to do, there is but one thing he *can* do; that is, move on toward the place of crucifixion. [E38]

——

I wonder whether God could make us understand all that happened there at the cross. [F68]

——

At the heart of the Christian system lies the cross of Christ with its divine paradox. [G11]

The cross stands in bold opposition to the natural man. [G11]

To try to find a common ground between the message of the cross and man's fallen reason is to try the impossible, and if persisted in must result in an impaired reason, a meaningless cross and a powerless Christianity. [G11]

Christ by His death on the cross made it possible for the sinner to exchange his sin for Christ's righteousness. [G32]

In coming to Christ we do not bring our old life up onto a higher plane; we leave it at the cross. The corn of wheat must fall into the ground and die. [H44]

The cross that ended the earthly life of Jesus now puts an end to the sinner; and the power that raised Christ from the dead now raises him to a new life along with Christ.

To any who may object to this or count it merely a narrow and private view of truth, let me say God has set His hallmark of approval upon this message from Paul's day to the present. Whether stated in these exact words or not, this has been the content of all preaching that has brought life and power to the world through the centuries. [H45]

Desire

In our desire after God let us keep always in mind that God also hath desire, and His desire is toward the sons of men, and more particularly toward those sons of men who will make the once-for-all decision to exalt Him over all. [A107]

———

Orthodox Christianity has fallen to its present low estate from lack of spiritual desire. Among the many who profess the Christian faith scarcely one in a thousand reveals any passionate thirst for God. [C56]

———

Whatever a man wants badly and persistently enough will determine the man's character. [C116]

———

Unsanctified desire will stop the growth of any Christian life. Wrong desire perverts the moral judgment so that we are unable to appraise the desired object at its real value. [C117]

———

Yet for all God's good will toward us He is unable to grant us our heart's desires till all our desires have been reduced to one. [D8]

Entertainment

... there are millions who cannot live without amusement; life without some form of entertainment for them is simply intolerable; they look forward to the blessed relief afforded by professional entertainers and other forms of psychological narcotics as a dope addict looks to his daily shot of heroin. [C31]

The abuse of a harmless thing is the essence of sin. The growth of the amusement phase of human life to such fantastic proportions is a portent, a threat to the souls of modern men. It has been built into a multimillion dollar racket with greater power over human minds and human character than any other educational influence on earth. [C32]

———

For centuries the Church stood solidly against every form of worldly entertainment, recognizing it for what it was—a device for wasting time, a refuge from the disturbing voice of conscience, a scheme to divert attention from moral accountability. [C32]

———

Many churches these days have become little more than poor theatres where fifth-rate "producers" peddle their shoddy wares with the full approval of evangelical leaders who can even quote a holy text in defense of their delinquency. And hardly a man dares raise his voice against it. [C33]

———

The great god Entertainment amuses his devotees mainly by telling them stories. The love of stories, which is a characteristic of childhood, has taken fast hold of the minds of the retarded saints of our day, so much so that not a few persons manage to make a comfortable living by spinning yarns and serving them up in various disguises to church people. What is natural and beautiful in a child may be shocking when it persists into

adulthood, and more so when it appears in the sanctuary
and seeks to pass for true religion. [C33]

———

If men do not have joy in their hearts they will seek it
somewhere else. If Christians are forbidden to enjoy the
wine of the Spirit they will turn to the wine of the
flesh for enjoyment. And that is exactly what
fundamental Christianity (as well as the so-called "full
gospel" groups) has done in the last quarter century.
God's people have turned to the amusements of the
world to try to squeeze a bit of juice out of them for the
relief of their dry and joyless hearts. "Gospel" boogie
singing now furnishes for many persons the only religious
joy they know. Others wipe their eyes tenderly over
"gospel" movies, and a countless number of amusements
flourish everywhere, paid for by the consecrated tithes
of persons who ought to know better. Our teachers took
away our right to be happy in God and the human heart
wreaked its terrible vengeance by going on a fleshly
binge from which the evangelical Church will not soon
recover, if indeed it ever does. [C69]

———

The whole religious machine has become a noisemaker.
The adolescent taste which loves the loud horn and
the thundering exhaust has gotten into the activities of
modern Christians. The old question, "What is the chief
end of man?" is now answered, "To dash about the
world and add to the din thereof." [C75]

———

The "Christian" film that seeks to draw customers by
picturing amorous love scenes in its advertising is

completely false to the religion of Chri.. spiritually blind will be taken in by it. [D38]

————

Today more than ever we Christians need to learn how to sanctify the ordinary. This is a blasé generation. People have been overstimulated to the place where their nerves are jaded and their tastes corrupted. Natural things have been rejected to make room for things artificial. The sacred has been secularized, the holy vulgarized and worship converted into a form of entertainment. [D68]

————

Our "vastly improved methods of communication" of which the shortsighted boast so loudly now enable a few men in strategic centers to feed into millions of minds alien thought stuff, ready-made and predigested. A little effortless assimilation of these borrowed ideas and the average man has done all the thinking he will or can do. This subtle brainwashing goes on day after day and year after year to the eternal injury of the populace—a populace, incidentally, which is willing to pay big money to have the job done, the reason being, I suppose, that it relieves them of the arduous and often frightening task of reaching independent decisions for which they must take responsibility. [E104]

————

No nation can long endure whose people have sold themselves for bread and circuses. [E105]

————

I have heard the notion seriously advanced that whereas once to win men to Christ it was necessary to have a gift from the Holy Spirit, now religious movies make it possible for anyone to win souls, without such spiritual anointing! "Whom the gods would destroy they first make mad." Surely such a notion is madness, but until now I have not heard it challenged among the evangelicals. [H66]

———

Godliness is no longer valued, except for the very old or the very dead. The saintly souls are forgotten in the whirl of religious activity. The noisy, the self-assertive, the entertaining are sought after and rewarded in every way, with gifts, crowds, offerings and publicity. The Christlike, the self-forgetting, the other-worldy are jostled aside to make room for the latest converted playboy who is usually not too well converted and still very much of a playboy. [H98]

———

It is now common practice in most evangelical churches to offer the people, especially the young people, a maximum of entertainment and a minimum of serious instruction. It is scarcely possible in most places to get anyone to attend a meeting where the only attraction is God. One can only conclude that God's professed children are bored with Him, for they must be wooed to meeting with a stick of striped candy in the form of religious movies, games and refreshments. [H136]

Eroticism

For millions the erotic has completely displaced the spiritual.

How the world got into this state is not difficult to trace. Contributing factors are the phonograph and radio, which can spread a love song from coast to coast within a matter of days; the motion picture and television, which enable a whole population to feast their eyes on sensuous women and amorous young men locked in passionate embrace (and this in the living room of "Christian" homes and before the eyes of innocent children!); shorter working hours and a multiplicity of mechanical gadgets with the resultant increased leisure for everyone. [D36]

———

The pure religion of Christ that flows like a crystal river from the heart of God is being polluted by the unclean waters that trickle from behind the altars of abomination that appear on every high hill and under every green tree from New York to Los Angeles.

The influence of the erotic spirit is felt almost everywhere in evangelical circles. Much of the singing in certain types of meetings has in it more of romance than it has of the Holy Ghost. Both words and music are designed to rouse the libidinous. Christ is courted with a familiarity that reveals a total ignorance of who He is. It is not the reverent intimacy of the adoring saint but the impudent familarity of the carnal lover.

Religious fiction also makes use of sex to interest the reading public, the paper-thin excuse being that if romance and religion are woven into a story the average person who would not read a purely religious book will read the story and thus be exposed to the gospel. Leaving aside the fact that most modern religious novelists are home talent amateurs, scarcely one of whom is capable of writing a single line of even fair literature, the whole concept behind the religio-romantic novel is unsound. [D38]

Eucharist

The communion will not have ultimate meaning for us if we do not believe that our Lord Jesus Christ is literally present in the Body of Christ on earth.

There is a distinction here: Christ is literally present with us—but not physically present. [K120]

___

Some people approach the communion table with an awe that is almost fear because they think they are approaching the physical presence of God. It is a mistake to imagine that He is physically present. [K120]

Experience

We are turning out from the Bible schools of this country year after year young men and women who know the theory of the Spirit-filled life but do not enjoy the experience. These go out into the churches to create in turn a generation of Christians who have never felt the power of the Spirit and who know nothing personally about the inner fire. [C88]

___

How long must we in America go on listening to men who can only tell us what they have read and heard about, never what they themselves have felt and heard and seen? [C88]

___

There are delights which the heart may enjoy in the awesome presence of God which cannot find expression in language; they belong to the unutterable element in

Christian experience. Not many enjoy them because not many know that they can. The whole concept of ineffable worship has been lost to this generation of Christians. C145

——

If only we would stop lamenting and look up. God is here. Christ is risen. The Spirit has been poured out from on high. All this we know as theological truth. It remains for us to turn it into joyous spiritual experience. And how is this accomplished? There is no new technique; if it is new it is false. The old, old method still works. Conscious fellowship with Christ is by faith, love and obedience. And the humblest believer need not be without these. G67

——

I make available here a little secret by which I have tested my own spiritual experiences and religious impulses for many years.

Briefly stated the test is this: This new doctrine, this new religious habit, this new view of truth, this new spiritual experience—*how has it affected my attitude toward and my relation to God, the Holy Scriptures, self, other Christians, the world and sin.* H121

——

I do not speak against the second work of grace; but I am pleading for the work that ought to be done in a man's heart when he first meets God. . . . Why should we be forced to invent some second or third or fourth experience somewhere along the line to obtain what we should have received the first time we met God? 135

64

Faith

At the root of the Christian life lies belief in the invisible.
The object of the Christian's faith is unseen reality. [A56]

———

Almost all who preach or write on the subject of faith
have much the same things to say concerning it. They
tell us that it is believing a promise, that it is taking
God at His word, that it is reckoning the Bible to be
true and stepping out upon it. The rest of the book or
sermon is usually taken up with stories of persons who
have had their prayers answered as a result of their faith.
These answers are mostly direct gifts of a practical and
temporal nature such as health, money, physical
protection or success in business. Or if the teacher is of
a philosophic turn of mind he may take another course
and lose us in a welter of metaphysics or snow us under
with psychological jargon as he defines and re-defines,
paring the slender hair of faith thinner and thinner till
it disappears in gossamer shavings at last. When he is
finished we get disappointed and go out "by that same
door where in we went." Surely there must be something
better than this. [A87]

———

. . . faith is the gaze of a soul upon a saving God. [A89]

———

. . . faith is not a once-done act, but a continuous gaze
of the heart at the Triune God. [A90]

———

Faith is the least self-regarding of the virtues. It is by its
very nature scarcely conscious of its own existence.

Like the eyes which sees everything in front of it and never sees itself, faith is occupied with the Object upon which it rests and pays no attention to itself at all. While we are looking at God we do not see ourselves— blessed riddance. The man who has struggled to purify himself and has had nothing but repeated failures will experience real relief when he stops tinkering with his soul and looks away to the perfect One. While he looks at Christ the very things he has so long been trying to do will be getting done within him. It will be God working in him to will and to do. [A91]

———

Faith is not in itself a meritorious act; the merit is in the One toward Whom it is directed. Faith is a re- directing of our sight, a getting out of the focus of our own vision and getting God into focus. [A91]

———

. . . if faith is the gaze of the heart at God, and if this gaze is but the raising of the inward eyes to meet the all-seeing eyes of God, then it follows that it is one of the easiest things possible to do. It would be like God to make the most vital thing easy and place it within the range of possibility for the weakest and poorest of us. [A94]

———

. . . the true quality of faith is almost universally missed, viz., its moral quality. [B38]

———

One marked difference between the faith of our fathers as conceived by the fathers and the same faith as understood and lived by their children is that the fathers were concerned with the root of the matter, while their present-day descendants seem concerned only with the fruit. C7

———

This generation of Christians must hear again the doctrine of the perturbing quality of faith. People must be told that the Christian religion is not something they can trifle with. The faith of Christ will command or it will have nothing to do with a man. It will not yield to experimentation. Its power cannot reach any man who is secretly keeping an escape route open in case things get too tough for him. The only man who can be sure he has true Bible faith is the one who has put himself in a position where he cannot go back. His faith has resulted in an everlasting and irrevocable committal, and however strongly he may be tempted he always replies, "Lord, to whom shall we go? thou hast the words of eternal life." C48

———

We can prove our faith by our committal to it, and in no other way. Any belief that does not command the one who holds it is not a real belief; it is a pseudo belief only. And it might shock some of us profoundly if we were brought suddenly face to face with our beliefs and forced to test them in the fires of practical living. C49

———

Pseudo faith always arranges a way out to serve in case God fails it. C50

———

Faith never means gullibility. The man who believes everything is as far from God as the man who refuses to believe anything. C120

It takes real faith to begin to live the life of heaven while still upon the earth, for this requires that we rise above the law of moral gravitation and bring to our everyday living the high wisdom of God. And since this wisdom is contrary to that of the world, conflict is bound to result. This, however, is a small price to pay for the inestimable privilege of following Christ. D98

———

Faith reposes on the character of God and if we believe that God is perfect we must conclude that His ways are perfect also. D117

———

Without faith it is impossible to please God, but not all faith pleases God. E54

———

True faith commits us to obedience. E57

———

Faith in faith is faith astray. E57

———

We must have faith; and let us not apologize for it, for faith is an organ of knowledge and can tell us more about ultimate reality than all the findings of science. We are not opposed to science, but we recognize its proper limitations and refuse to stop where it is compelled to stop. The Bible tells of another world too fine for the instruments of scientific research to discover. By faith we engage that world and make it ours. It is accessible to us through the blood of the everlasting covenant. If we will believe we may even now enjoy the presence of God and the ministry of His heavenly messengers. Only unbelief can rob us of this royal privilege. [E118]

————

There is about the Christian faith a quiet dogmatism, a cheerful intolerance. It feels no need to appease its enemies or compromise with its detractors. Christ came from God, out of eternity, to report on the things He had seen and heard and to establish true values for the confused human race. [E129]

————

The Christian faith engages the profoundest problems the human mind can entertain and solves them completely and simply by pointing to the Lamb of God. [E129]

————

God's eternity and man's mortality join to persuade us that faith in Jesus Christ is not optional. For every man it must be Christ or eternal tragedy. [F48]

————

Faith is not optimism, though it may breed optimism; it is not cheerfulness, though the man of faith is likely to be a reasonably cheerful; it is not a vague sense of well-being or a tender appreciation for the beauty of human togetherness. Faith is confidence in God's self-revelation as found in the Holy Scriptures. [G51]

————

The contemporary moral climate does not favor a faith as tough and fibrous as that taught by our Lord and His apostles. [G76]

When faith gains the consent of the will to make an
irrevocable committal to Christ as Lord, truth begins its
saving, illuminating work; and not one moment before. [G93]

———

In natural matters faith follows evidence and is
impossible without it, but in the realm of the spirit faith
precedes understanding; it does not follow it. The natural
man must know in order to believe; the spiritual man
must believe in order to know. The faith that saves
is not a conclusion drawn from evidence; it is a moral
thing, a thing of the spirit, a supernatural infusion of
confidence in Jesus Christ, a very gift of God. [I129]

———

In the divine scheme of salvation the doctrine of faith
is central. God addresses His words to faith, and where
no faith is no true revelation is possible, "*Without faith
it is impossible to please him.*" [H31]

———

Faith as the Bible knows it is confidence in God and
His Son Jesus Christ; it is the response of the soul to
the divine character as revealed in the Scriptures; and
even this response is impossible apart from the prior
inworking of the Holy Spirit. Faith is a gift of God to a
penitent soul and has nothing whatsoever to do with
the senses or the data they afford. Faith is a miracle; it
is the ability God gives to trust His Son, and anything
that does not result in action in accord with the will
of God is not faith but something else short of it. [H33]

Faith and morals are two sides of the same coin. Indeed the very essence of faith is moral. Any professed faith in Christ as personal Saviour that does not bring the life under plenary obedience to Christ as Lord is inadequate and must betray its victim at the last. [H33]

———

The man that believes will obey; failure to obey is convincing proof that there is not true faith present. To attempt the impossible God must give faith or there will be none, and He gives faith to the obedient heart only. [H33]

———

True faith brings a spiritual and moral transformation and an inward witness that cannot be mistaken. These come when we stop believing in belief and start believing in the Lord Jesus Christ indeed. [H61]

———

When men believe God they speak boldly. When they doubt they confer. Much current religious talk is but uncertainty rationalizing itself; and this they call "engaging in the contemporary dialogue." [H115]

———

The world has nothing that we want—for we are believers in a faith that is as well authenticated as any solid fact of life. The truths we believe and the links in the chain of evidence are clear and rational. I contend that the church has a right to rejoice and that this is no time in the world's history for Christian believers to settle for a defensive holding action! [134]

Let me warn you that if you are a Christian believer and you have found a psychologist who can explain to you exactly what happened to you in the matter of your faith, you have been unfrocked! At the very moment that a man's experience in Christ can be broken down and explained by the psychologists, we have just another church member on our hands—and not a believing Christian! [138]

Forgiveness

The idea that God will pardon a rebel who has not given up his rebellion is contrary both to the Scriptures and to common sense. [C43]

———

I believe that the chronic unhappiness of most Christians may be attributed to a gnawing uneasiness lest God has not fully forgiven them, or the fear that He expects as the price of His forgiveness some sort of emotional penance which they have not furnished. [G99]

———

To be forgiven, a sin must be forsaken. [H64]

Freedom

The important thing about a man is not where he goes when he is compelled to go, but where he goes when he is free to go where he will. [H158]

The true character of a people is revealed in the uses it makes of its freedoms. [H159]

———

It is the free nation that reveals its character by its voluntary choices. The man who "bowed by the weight of centuries. . .leans upon his hoe and gazes on the ground" when the long day's work is over is glad to get home to supper and to bed; he has little time for anything else. But in those fortunate lands where modern machinery and labor unions have given men many free hours out of every day and at least two free days out of every week, they have time to do almost anything they will. They are free to destroy themselves by their choices, and many of them are doing just that. [H159]

———

Any nation which for an extended period puts pleasure before liberty is likely to lose the liberty it misused. [H159]

———

I think it might be well for us to check our spiritual condition occasionally by the simple test of compatibility. When we are free to go, where do we go? In what company do we feel most at home? Where do our thoughts turn when they are free to turn where they will? When the pressure of work or business or school has temporarily lifted and we are able to think of what we will instead of what we must, what do we think of then? [H160]

———

. . . if man's will is not free to do evil, it is not free to do good!

The freedom of human will is necessary to the concept of morality. [K87]

Friends

Unquestionably the highest privilege granted to man on earth is to be admitted into the circle of the friends of God. Nothing is important enough to be allowed to stand in the way of our relation to God. [G121]

———

God is not satisfied until there exists between Him and His people a relaxed informality that requires no artificial stimulation. The true friend of God may sit in His presence for long periods in silence. Complete trust needs no words of assurance. [G121]

———

True friends trust each other. [G121]

———

To seek to be friends with those who will not be the friends of Christ is to be a traitor to our Lord. [H168]

Fundamentalism

Fundamentalism has stood aloof from the Liberal in self-conscious superiority and has on its own part fallen into error, the error of textualism, which is simply orthodoxy without the Holy Ghost. Everywhere among Conservatives we find persons who are Bible-taught but not Spirit-taught. [B78]

It was religion that put Christ on the cross, religion without the indwelling Spirit. It is no use to deny that Christ was crucified by persons who would today be called Fundamentalists. B103'

____

We evangelicals have become sophisticated, blasé. We have lost what someone called the "millennial component" from our Christian faith. To escape what we believe to be the slough of a mistaken hope we have detoured far out into the wilderness of complete hopelessness. H153

____

Little by little evangelical Christians these days are being brainwashed. One evidence is that increasing numbers of them are becoming ashamed to be found unequivocally on the side of truth. They say they believe but their beliefs have been so diluted as to be impossible of clear definition. H164

Gifts and Giving

There is a place in the religious experience where we love God for Himself alone, with never a thought of His benefits. C149

____

Among the gifts of the Spirit scarcely any one is of greater practical usefulness than the gift of discernment. This gift should be highly valued and frankly sought as being almost indispensable in these critical times. This gift will enable us to distinguish the chaff from the wheat and to divide the manifestations of the flesh from the operations of the Spirit. [C153]

———

"For Thy sake" will rescue the little, empty things from vanity and give them eternal meaning. [D70]

———

To God there are no small offerings if they are made in the name of His Son. [D71]

———

Left to ourselves we tend immediately to reduce God to manageable terms. We want to get Him where we can use Him, or at least know where He is when we need Him. [F16]

———

Not by its size is my gift judged, but by how much of me there is in it. No man gives at all until he has given all. No man gives anything acceptable to God until he has first given himself in love and sacrifice. [G105]

———

It is right that we should tithe because it is God's work, but it does not really cost us anything—it does not bring us to the point of sacrificial giving. [J70]

God

What a broad world to roam in, what a sea to swim in this God and Father of our Lord Jesus Christ. [A39]

God is so vastly wonderful, so utterly and completely delightful that He can, without anything other than Himself, meet and overflow the deepest demands of our total nature, mysterious and deep as that nature is. [A42]

———

. . . God is real. He is real in the absolute and final sense that nothing else is. All other reality is contingent upon His. The great Reality is God who is the Author of that lower and dependent reality which makes up the sum of created things, including ourselves. God has objective existence independent of and apart from any notions which we may have concerning Him. The worshipping heart does not create its Object. It finds Him here when it wakes from its moral slumber in the morning of its regeneration. [A55]

———

So let us begin with God. Back of all, above all, before all is God; first in sequential order, above in rank and station, exalted in dignity and honor. As the self-existent One He gave being to all things, and all things exist out of Him and for Him. [A101]

———

God was our original habitat and our hearts cannot but feel at home when they enter again that ancient and beautiful abode. [A104]

———

Nothing will or can restore order till our hearts make the great decision; God shall be exalted above. [A105]

For all things God is the great Antecedent. Because He
is, we are and everything else is. He is that "dread,
unbeginning One," self-caused, self-contained and self-
sufficient. [B20]

———

We cannot think rightly of God until we begin to think
of Him as always being *there*, and *there first*. [B20]

———

Begin where we will, God is there first. [B21]

———

God in His essential Being is unique in the only sense
that word will bear. That is, there is nothing like Him
in the universe. What He is cannot be conceived by the
mind because He is "altogether other" than anything
with which we have had experience before. The mind
has no material with which to start. No man has ever
entertained a thought which can be said to describe
God in any but the vaguest and most imperfect sense.
Where God is known at all it must be otherwise than
by our creature-reason. [B95]

———

God is not contained: He contains. [D120]

———

Always God must be first [E110]

———

. . . the Christian conception of God current in these
middle years of the twentieth century is so decadent as

to be utterly beneath the dignity of the Most High God and actually to constitute for professed believers something amounting to a moral calamity. [F10]

Origin is a word that can apply only to things created. When we think of anything that has origin we are not thinking of God. God is self-existent, while all created things necessarily originated somewhere at some time. Aside from God, nothing is self-caused. [F33]

The human mind, being created, has an understandable uneasiness about the Uncreated. We do not find it comfortable to allow for the presence of One who is wholly outside of the circle of our familiar knowledge. We tend to be disquieted by the thought of One who does not account to us for His being, who is responsible to no one, who is self-existent, self-dependent and self-sufficient. [F33]

It may be stated as an axiom that to stay alive every created thing needs some other created thing and all things need God. To God alone nothing is necessary. [F40]

. . . were every man on earth to become atheist, it could not affect God in any way. He is what He is in Himself without regard to any other. To believe in Him adds nothing to His perfections; to doubt Him takes nothing away. [F40]

God never hurries. There are no deadlines against which He must work. [F53]

God knows instantly and effortlessly all matter and all matters, all mind and every mind, all spirit and all spirits, all being and every being, all creaturehood and all creatures, every plurality and all pluralities, all law and every law, all relations, all causes, all thoughts, all mysteries, all enigmas, all feeling, all desires, every unuttered secret, all thrones and dominions, all personalities, all things visible and invisible in heaven and in earth, motion, space, time, life, death, good, evil, heaven, and hell. [F62]

———

God is spirit, and to Him magnitude and distance have no meaning. To us they are useful as analogies and illustrations, so God refers to them constantly when speaking down to our limited understanding. [F75]

———

God is a Person and can be known in increasing degrees of intimate acquaintance as we prepare our hearts for the wonder. It may be necessary for us to alter our former beliefs about God as the glory that gilds the Sacred Scriptures dawns over our interior lives. We may also need to break quietly and graciously with the lifeless textualism that prevails among the gospel churches, and to protest the frivolous character of much that passes for Christianity among us. [F123]

———

... the great devotional theologians of the centuries taught the futility of trying to visualize the Godhead. [G91]

Some things are not debatable; there is no other side to them. There is only God's side. [H114]

———

God being who He is, the inheritance we receive from Him is limitless—it is all of the universe! [174]

———

Anyone who knows God, even slightly, would expect God to make an orderly world because God Himself is the essence of order. God was never the author of disorder—whether it be in society, in the home, or in the mind or body of man. [190]

God and Man

Until a man has gotten into trouble with his heart he is not likely to get out of trouble with God. [C39]

———

A man by his sin may waste himself, which is to waste that which on earth is most like God. This is man's greatest tragedy, God's heaviest grief. [C99]

———

Man in the plan of God has been permitted considerable say; but never is he permitted to utter the first word nor the last. That is the prerogative of the Deity, and one which He will never surrender to His creatures. [C158]

———

To know man we must begin with God. [D20]

We try to climb up to high position when God has
ordained that we go down. [D51]

———

It is dissimilarity that creates the sense of remoteness
between creatures and between men and God. [D121]

———

No man should desire to be happy who is not at the
same time holy. He should spend his efforts in seeking
to know and do the will of God, leaving to Christ the
matter of how happy he shall be. [E46]

———

We naturally and correctly think of man as a work
wrought by the divine Intelligence. He is both created
and made. How he was created lies undisclosed among
the secrets of God; how he was brought from not-being
to being, from no-thing to some-thing is not known
and may never be known to any but the One who
brought him forth. How God *made* him, however, is
less of a secret, and while we know only a small portion
of the whole truth, we do know that man possesses a
body, a soul, and a spirit; we know that he has memory,
reason, will, intelligence, sensation, and we know that
to give these meaning he has the wondrous gift of
consciousness. We know, too, that these, together with
various qualities of temperament, compose his total
human self. These are gifts from God arranged by infinite
wisdom, notes that make up the score of creation's
loftiest symphony, threads that compose the master
tapestry of the universe. [F23]

. . . the marks of God's image in man is his ability to exercise moral choice. The teaching of Christianity is that man chose to be independent of God and confirmed his choice by deliberately disobeying a divine command. This act violated the relationship that normally existed between God and His creature; it rejected God as the ground of existence and threw man back upon himself. Thereafter he became not a planet revolving around the central Sun, but a sun in his own right, around which everything else must revolve. [F36]

———

The Christian religion has to do with God and man, but its focal point is God, not man. Man's only claim to importance is that he was created in the divine image; in himself he is nothing. [F42]

———

The old man, even at his best, possesses only the life of Adam: the new man has the life of God. And this is more than a mere manner of speaking; it is quite literally true. When God infuses eternal life into the spirit of a man, the man becomes a member of a new and higher order of being. [F58]

———

Until we have seen ourselves as God sees us, we are not likely to be much disturbed over conditions around us as long as they do not get so far out of hand as to threaten our comfortable way of life. [F110]

———

When Jesus walked on earth He was a man acting like God; but equally wonderful is it that He was also God acting like Himself in man and in a man. [G39]

And what kind of habitation pleases God? What must
our natures be like before He can feel at home within
us? He asks nothing but a pure heart and a single mind.
He asks no rich paneling, no rugs from the Orient, no
art treasures from afar. He desires but sincerity,
transparency, humility and love. He will see to the rest. G43

———

God and man exist for each other and neither is satisfied
without the other. G83

———

Even among those who acknowledge the deity of Christ
there is often a failure to recognize His manhood. We
are quick to assert that when He walked the earth he
was *God with men*, but we overlook a truth equally as
important, that where He sits now on His mediatorial
throne He is *Man with God*. H141

———

The argument of the apostles is that the Man Jesus has
been made higher than angels, higher than Moses and
Aaron, higher than any creature in earth or heaven. And
this exalted position He attained *as a man*. As God He
already stood infinitely above all other beings. No
argument was needed to prove the transcendence of the
Godhead. The apostles were not declaring the
preeminence of God, which would have been superfluous,
but of a man, which was necessary. H143

———

God shines in many ways throughout His universe . . .
He shines best of all in the lives of men and women He
created and then redeemed. J166

Fear of God

No one can know the true grace of God who has not first known the fear of God. C38

———

The saving power of the Word is reserved for those for whom it is intended. The secret of the Lord is with them that fear Him. H28

———

. . . the good Christian is in love with one he has never seen, and although he fears and reveres God, he is not afraid of God at all! I142

Glory of God

God's glory is and must forever remain the Christian's true point of departure. Anything that begins anywhere else, whatever it is, is certainly not New Testament Christianity. D23

———

The heavens and the earth were intended to be a semitransparent veil through which moral intelligences might see the glory of God, but for sin-blinded men this veil has become opaque. They see the creation but do not see through it to the Creator; or what glimpses they do have are dim and out of focus. It is possible to spend a lifetime admiring God's handiwork without acknowledging the presence of the God whose handiwork it is. E114

. . . everything God does is praiseworthy and deserves our deepest admiration. Whether He is making or redeeming a world, He is perfect in all His doings and glorious in all His goings forth. [E119]

———

The Glory of God has not been revealed to this generation of men. The God of contemporary Christianity is only slightly superior to the gods of Greece and Rome, if indeed He is not actually inferior to them in that He is weak and helpless while they at least had power. [F16]

Goodness of God

The fellowship of God is delightful beyond all telling. He communes with His redeemed ones in an easy, uninhibited fellowship that is restful and healing to the soul. He is not sensitive nor selfish nor temperamental. What He is today we shall find Him tomorrow and the next day and the next year. He is not hard to please, though He may be hard to satisfy. He expects of us only what He has Himself first supplied. He is quick to mark every simple effort to please Him, and just as quick to overlook imperfections when He knows we meant to do His will. He loves us for ourselves and values our love more than galaxies of new created worlds. [C15]

———

God is the sum of all patience and the essence of kindly good will. We please Him most, not by frantically trying to make ourselves good, but by throwing ourselves into His arms with all our imperfections, and believing that He understands everything and loves us still. [C15]

With the goodness of God to desire our highest welfare, the wisdom of God to plan it, and the power of God to achieve it, what do we lack? Surely we are the most favored of all creatures. [F70]

———

God, being who He is, cannot cease to what He is, and being what He is, He cannot act out of character with Himself. He is at once faithful and immutable, so all His words and acts must be and must remain faithful. Men become unfaithful out of desire, fear, weakness, loss of interest, or because of some strong influence from without. Obviously none of these forces can affect God in any way. He is His own reason for all He is and does. He cannot be compelled from without, but ever speaks and acts from within Himself by His own sovereign will as it pleases Him. [F83]

———

Upon God's faithfulness rests our whole hope of future blessedness. Only as He is faithful will His covenants stand and His promises be honored. Only as we have complete assurance that He is faithful may we live in peace and look forward with assurance to the life to come. [F87]

———

Divine goodness, as one of God's attributes, is self-caused, infinite, perfect, and eternal. Since God is immutable He never varies in the intensity of His loving-kindness. He has never been kinder than He now is, nor will He ever be less kind. [F89]

God's compassion flows out of His goodness, and goodness without justice is not goodness. God spares us because He is good, but He could not be good if He were not just. [F94]

———

Grace is the good pleasure of God that inclines Him to bestow benefits upon the undeserving. It is a self-existent principle inherent in the divine nature and appears to us as a self-caused propensity to pity the wretched, spare the guilty, welcome the outcast, and bring into favor those who were before under just disapprobation. Its use to us sinful men is to save us and make us sit together in heavenly places to demonstrate to the ages the exceeding riches of God's kindness to us in Christ Jesus. [F100]

Image of God

God has made us in His likeness, and one mark of that likeness is our free will. [B49]

———

Everything that God does in His ransomed children has as its long range purpose the final restoration of the divine image in human nature. Everything looks forward to the consummation. [C60]

———

The widest thing in the universe is not space; it is the potential capacity of the human heart. Being made in the image of God, it is capable of almost unlimited extension in all directions. And one of the world's worst tragedies is that we allow our hearts to shrink until there is room in them for little beside ourselves. C112

——

. . . one soul made in the image of God is more precious to Him than all the starry universe. Astronomy deals with space and matter and motion; theology deals with life and personality and the mystery of being. D75

——

The yearning to know what cannot be known, to comprehend the Incomprehensible, to touch and taste the Unapproachable, arises from the image of God in the nature of man. F17

——

. . . because we are the handiwork of God, it follows that _all our problems and their solutions are theological_. Some knowledge of what kind of God it is that operates the universe is indispensable to a sound philosophy of life and a sane outlook on the world scene. F34

——

Only that creature whom he called "man" did God make in His own image and likeness. So, when man failed and sinned and fell, God said, "I will go down now." J108

Immutability of God

The immutability of God appears in its most perfect beauty when viewed against the mutability of men. In God no change is possible; in men change is impossible to escape. Neither the man is fixed nor his world, but

he and it are in constant flux. Each man appea₋
a little while to laugh and weep, to work and play, and
then to go to make room for those who shall follow
him in the never-ending cycle. [F56]

———

God never changes moods or cools off in His affections
or loses enthusiasm. [F59]

———

The truth is that there is not and can never be anything
outside of the nature of God which can move Him in
the least degree. All God's reasons come from within
His uncreated being. Nothing has entered the being of
God from eternity, nothing has been removed, and
nothing has been changed. [F93]

Knowledge of God

. . . the man who would know God must give time to
Him. [B22]

———

The Christian is strong or weak depending upon how
closely he has cultivated the knowledge of God. [C11]

———

God can be known satisfactorily only as we devote time
to Him. [C12]

———

God will respond to our efforts to know Him. [C13]

We can never know who or what we are till we know at least something of what God is. [F35]

———

To know God is at once the easiest and the most difficult thing in the world. It is easy because the knowledge is not won by hard mental toil, but is something freely given. [F122]

———

God always acts like Himself, wherever He may be and whatever He may be doing; in Him there is neither variableness nor shadow of turning. Yet His infinitude places Him so far above our knowing that a lifetime spent in cultivating the knowledge of Him leaves as much yet to learn as if we had never begun.

God's limitless knowledge and perfect wisdom enable Him to work rationally beyond the bounds of our rational knowing. For this reason we cannot predict God's actions as we can predict the movements of the heavenly bodies, so He constantly astonishes us as He moves in freedom through His universe. So imperfectly do we know Him that it may be said that one invariable concomitant of a true encounter with God is delighted wonder. No matter how high our expectation may be, when God finally moves into the field of our spiritual awareness we are sure to be astonished by His power to overwhelm the mind and fascinate the soul. [G38]

Love of God

The phrase "the love of God," when used by Christians, almost always refers to God's love for us. We must remember that it can also mean our love for God. [C147]

The deep, deep love of God is the fountain out of which flows our future beatitude, and the grace of God in Christ is the channel by which it reaches us. [D137]

———

Equating love with God is a major mistake which has produced much unsound religious philosophy and has brought forth a spate of vaporous poetry completely out of accord with the Holy Scriptures and altogether of another climate from that of historic Christianity. [F104]

———

If literally God is love, then literally love is God, and we are in all duty bound to worship love as the only God there is. If love is equal to God then God is only equal to love, and God and love are identical. Thus we destroy the concept of personality in God and deny outright all His attributes save one, and that one we substitute for God. [F104]

———

The words "God is love" mean that love is an essential attribute of God. Love is something true of God but it is not God. It expresses the way God is in His unitary being, as do the words holiness, justice, faithfulness and truth. Because God is immutable He always acts like Himself, and because He is a unity He never suspends one of His attributes in order to exercise another. [F105]

———

From God's other known attributes we may learn much about His love. We can know, for instance, that because God is self-existent, His love had no beginning; because

He is eternal, His love can have no end; because He is
infinite, it has no limit; because He is holy, it is the
quintessence of all spotless purity; because He is
immense, His love is an incomprehensibly vast,
bottomless, shoreless sea before which we kneel in
joyful silence and from which the loftiest eloquence
retreats confused and abashed. [F105]

——

It is a strange and beautiful eccentricity of the free God
that He has allowed His heart to be emotionally identified
with men. Self-sufficient as He is, He wants our love
and will not be satisfied till He gets it. Free as He is,
He has let His heart be bound to us forever. [F107]

——

The love of God is one of the great realities of the
universe, a pillar upon which the hope of the world rests.
But it is a personal, intimate thing, too. God does not
love populations, He loves people. He loves not masses,
but men. He loves us all with a mighty love that has
no beginning and can have no end. [F109]

Mercy of God

Mercy is an attribute of God, an infinite and inexhaustible
energy within the divine nature which disposes God to
be actively compassionate. [F96]

——

Were there no guilt in the world, no pain and no tears,
God would yet be infinitely merciful; but His mercy
might well remain hidden in His heart, unknown to the
created universe. No voice would be raised to celebrate

the mercy of which none felt the need. It is human misery and sin that call forth the divine mercy. [F97]

——

We do believe in justice and we do believe in judgment. We believe the only reason mercy triumphs over judgment is that God, by a divine, omniscient act of redemption, fixed it so man could escape justice and live in the sea of mercy. The justified man, the man who believes in Jesus Christ, born anew and now a redeemed child of God, lives in that mercy always. [155]

Power of God

It is hard for us sons of the Machine Age to remember that there is no power apart from God. Whether physical, intellectual, moral or spiritual, power is contained in God, flows out from Him, and returns to Him again. The power that works throughout His creation remains in Him even while it operates in an atom or a galaxy. [D24]

——

Whatever God is He is infinitely. In Him lies all the power there is; any power at work anywhere is His. Even the power to do evil must first have come from Him since there is no other source from which it could come. [D26]

——

If we miss seeing God in His works we deprive ourselves of the sight of a royal display of wisdom and power so elevating, so ennobling, so awe-inspiring as to make all attempts at description futile. Such a sight the angels behold day and night forever and ask nothing more to make them perpetually satisfied. [E119]

Omnipotence is not a name given to the sum of all power, but an attribute of a personal God whom we Christians believe to be the Father of our Lord Jesus Christ and of all who believe on Him to life eternal. The worshiping man finds this knowledge a source of wonderful strength for his inner life. His faith rises to take the great leap upward into the fellowship of Him who can do whatever He wills to do, for whom nothing is hard or difficult because He possesses power absolute. [F73]

Presence of God

At the heart of the Christian message is God Himself waiting for His redeemed children to push in to conscious awareness of His Presence. [A37]

The world is perishing for lack of the knowledge of God and the Church is famishing for want of His Presence. The instant cure of most of our religious ills would be to enter the Presence in spiritual experience, to become suddenly aware that we are in God and that God is in us. This would lift us out of our pitiful narrowness and cause our hearts to be enlarged. [A38]

A spiritual kingdom lies all about us, enclosing us, embracing us, altogether within reach of our inner selves, waiting for us to recognize it. God Himself is here waiting our response to His Presence. This eternal world will come alive to us the moment we begin to reckon upon its reality. [A52]

Wherever we are, God is here. There is no place, there can be no place, where He is not. Ten million intelligences standing at as many points in space and separated by incomprehensible distances can each one say with equal truth, God is here. No point is nearer to God than any other point. It is exactly as near to God from any place as it is from any other place. No one is in mere distance any further from or any nearer to God than any other person is. A62

Adam sinned and, in his panic, frantically tried to do the impossible; he tried to hide from the Presence of God. A63

The Universal Presence is a fact. God is here. The whole universe is alive with His life. And He is no strange or foreign God, but the familiar Father of our Lord Jesus Christ whose love has for these thousands of years enfolded the sinful race of men. And always He is trying to get our attention, to reveal Himself to us, to communicate with us. We have within us the ability to know Him if we will but respond to His overtures. A71

Nothing can take the place of the *touch* of God in the soul and the sense of Someone there. B25

God is altogether present wherever He is present at all. B73

The best way to keep the enemy out is to keep Christ in. The sheep need not be terrified by the wolf; they have but to stay close to the shepherd. It is not the praying sheep Satan fears but the presence of the shepherd. D43

———

In God there is no *was* or *will be*, but a continuous and unbroken *is*. In Him history and prophecy are one and the same. D115

———

We look forward to events predicted and backward to events that have occurred; but God contains past and future in His own all-encompassing Being. To Him every event has already occurred, or perhaps it would be more accurate to say it is occurring. With Him there can never be a memory of things past nor an expectation of things to come, but only a knowledge of all things past and future as instantaneously present before His mind. D115

———

The God of Abraham has withdrawn His conscious Presence from us, and another God whom our fathers knew not is making himself at home among us. This God we have made and because we have made him we can understand him; because we have created him he can never surprise us, never overwhelm us, nor astonish us, nor transcend us. F49

———

The certainty that God is always near us, present in all parts of His world, closer to us than our thoughts, should maintain us in a state of high moral happiness most of the time. But not all the time. It would be less than honest to promise every believer continual jubilee and less than realistic to expect it. F82

———

My fellow man, do you not know that your great sin is this: the all-pervading and eternal Presence is here, and you cannot feel Him? J89

———

Why doesn't the sky fall down? Why is it that stars and planets do not go tearing apart and ripping off into chaos?

Because there is a Presence that makes all things consist—and it is the Presence of that One who upholdeth all things by the word of His power. This is basically a spiritual explanation, for this universe can only be explained by spiritual and eternal laws. J97

———

Wherever people are gathered together in the Name, there also is the Presence. So it is that the Presence and the Name constitute the true assembly of believers and it is recognized by God in heaven. K48

———

It is not the form that makes the church or its service. The Presence and the Name—these make the church. K48

Pursuit of God

We pursue God because, and only because, He has first put an urge within us that spurs us to the pursuit. A11

If we would find God amid all the religious externals we must first determine to find Him, and then proceed in the way of simplicity. Now as always God discovers Himself to "babes" and hides Himself in thick darkness from the wise and the prudent. We must simplify our approach to Him. We must strip down to essentials (and they will be found to be blessedly few). We must put away all effort to impress, and come with the guileless candor of childhood. If we do this, without doubt God will quickly respond. A18

————

We need not fear that in seeking God only we may narrow our lives or restrict the motions of our expanding hearts. The opposite is true. We can well afford to make God our All, to concentrate, to sacrifice the many for the One. A18

————

God formed us for His pleasure, and so formed us that we as well as He can in divine communion enjoy the sweet and mysterious mingling of kindred personalities. He meant us to see Him and live with Him and draw our life from His smile. A34

————

Our pursuit of God is successful just because He is forever seeking to manifest Himself to us. A65

————

What God in His sovereignty may yet do on a world-scale I do not claim to know: but what He will do for the plain man or woman who seeks His face I believe I do know and can tell others. Let any man turn to God in earnest, let him begin to exercise himself unto godliness, let him seek to develop his powers of spiritual receptivity by trust and obedience and humility, and the results will exceed anything he may have hoped in his leaner and weaker days. A71

———

When the habit of inwardly gazing Godward becomes fixed within us we shall be ushered onto a new level of spiritual life more in keeping with the promises of God and the mood of the New Testament. The Triune God will be our dwelling place even while our feet walk the low road of simple duty here among men. A97

———

Much of our difficulty as seeking Christians stems from our unwillingness to take God as He is and adjust our lives accordingly. We insist upon trying to modify Him and to bring Him nearer to our own image. A101

———

The man who has met God is not looking for something— he has found it; he is not searching for light—upon him the Light has already shined. C157

———

We are called to an everlasting preoccupation with God. G46

———

God is never found accidentally. "Ye shall seek me, and find me, when ye shall search for me with all your heart." H56

The man that has the most of God is the man who is seeking the most ardently for more of God. [H106]

Voice of God

God is speaking. Not God spoke, but God *is speaking.* He is by His nature continuously articulate. He fills the world with His speaking Voice. [A73]

———

The Bible is the written word of God, and because it is written it is confined and limited by the necessities of ink and paper and leather. The Voice of God, however, is alive and free as the sovereign God is free. *"The words that I speak unto you, they are spirit, and they are life."* The life is in the speaking words. God's word in the Bible can have power only because it corresponds to God's word in the universe. It is the present Voice which makes the written Word all-powerful. Otherwise it would lie locked in slumber within the covers of a book. [A74]

———

That God is here and that He is speaking—these truths are back of all other Bible truths; without them there could be no revelation at all. God did not write a book and send it by messenger to be read at a distance by unaided minds. He spoke a Book and lives in His spoken words, constantly speaking His words and causing the power of them to persist across the years. [A75]

———

The Word of God is quick and powerful. In the beginning He spoke to nothing, and it became *something.* Chaos heard it and became order, darkness heard it and became light. "*And God said—and it was so.*" The twin phrases, as cause and effect, occur throughout the Genesis story of the creation. The *said* accounts for the *so*. The *so* is the *said* put into the continuous present. [A75]

———

The Voice of God is a friendly Voice. No one need fear to listen to it unless he has already made up his mind to resist it. [A80]

———

Whoever will listen will hear the speaking Heaven. This is definitely not the hour when men take kindly to an exhortation to *listen*, for listening is not today a part of popular religion. We are at the opposite end of the pole from there. Religion has accepted the monstrous heresy that noise, size, activity and bluster make a man dear to God. [A80]

The Bible will never be a living Book to us until we are convinced that God is articulate in His universe. [A81]

Will of God

To will the will of God is to do more than give unprotesting consent to it; it is rather to choose God's will with positive determination. [B105]

———

... thank God you don't have to be flawless to be blessed!

You need to have a big heart that desires and wants
the will of God more than anything else in the world.
You need also to have an eye single to His glory. [K19]

————

I believe God wants to do something new and blessed
for every believer who has the inner desire to know
Him better. I am aware of the fact that it takes a store
of patience and persistence and a lot of courage to find
and pursue the will of God in this day. [K65]

————

There is no religious group or church organization or
denominational communion in the world that God will
not desert and abandon in the very hour it ceases to
fulfill and carry out His divine will. [K65]

————

There is no possible way that ecclesiastical robes are
impressive enough nor cross and chains heavy enough
nor titles long enough to save the church when once
she ceases to fulfill the will of God among sinful men
who need the transforming news of Christ's gospel. [K66]

————

If we do not make a hard swing back to the very roots
of Christian faith and Christian teaching and Christian
living, beginning again to seek the face of God and His
will, God is going to pass us up! [K67]

————

Our Lord Jesus Christ had no secondary aims. His one
passion in life was the fulfillment of His Father's will. [K123]

Gospel

We must constantly keep in mind that the gospel is not good news only, but a judgment as well upon everyone that hears it. The message of the Cross is good news indeed for the penitent, but to those who "obey not the gospel" it carries an overtone of warning. [B35]

——

For sinners who want to cease being willful sinners and become obedient children of God the gospel message is one of unqualified peace, but it is by its very nature also an arbiter of the future destinies of men. [B35]

——

The Christian message rightly understood means this: The God who by the *word* of the gospel *proclaims* men free, by the *power* of the gospel *actually makes them free*. To accept less than this is to know the gospel in word only, without its power. [B39]

——

The message of the gospel . . . is the message of a new creation in the midst of an old, the message of the invasion of our human nature by the eternal life of God and the displacing of the old by the new. [B42]

——

The Gospel not only furnishes transforming power to remold the human heart; it provides also a model after which the new life is to be fashioned, and that model is Christ Himself. Christ is God acting like God in the lowly raiments of human flesh. [C59]

The gospel in its scriptural context puts the glory of God first and the salvation of man second. [D23]

———

The glory of the gospel is its freedom. [E73]

———

... the blessed news is that the God who needs no one has in sovereign condescension stooped to work by and in and through His obedient children. [F43]

———

The witness of the church is most effective when she declares rather than explains, for the gospel is addressed not to reason but to faith. [G11]

———

One of the glories of the Christian gospel is its ability not only to deliver a man from sin but to orient him to place him on a peak from which he can see yesterday and today in their relation to tomorrow. [H94]

Greatness

... true greatness lies in character, not in ability or position. [D51]

———

Many people in our day seem to dream of becoming great while there are far too few who spend any time in concern about being good. [J25]

If a poll should be taken today to name the six greatest
men in the world and our names would not be included,
we would still have the same privileges in God's world
that they would have! We can breathe God's beautiful
air, look at His blue sky, gaze into a never-ending array
of stars in the night sky. We can stand upon the hard
earth and stamp our little feet—and our big feet, too—
and know that it will sustain us. We are as much a part
of this human race as the greatest men and women. [K52]

——

I believe there is something inherent in human greatness
and fame and recognition that works subtly against the
quality of fine spiritual insight in the human mind.
World leaders as a rule do not possess spiritual insight. [J64]

Happiness

The man who really knows himself can never believe
in his right to be happy. A little glimpse of his own heart
will disillusion him instantly so that he is more likely
to turn on himself and own God's sentence against him
to be just. The doctrine of man's inalienable right to
happiness is anti-God and anti-Christ, and its wide
acceptance by society tells us a lot about that same
society. [E45]

——

There is an ignoble pursuit of irresponsible happiness
among us. [H104]

I do not believe that it is the will of God that we should seek to be happy, but rather that we should seek to be holy and useful. [H104]

————

When the followers of Jesus Christ lose their interest in heaven they will no longer be happy Christians and when they are no longer happy Christians they cannot be a powerful force in a sad and sinful world. [J105]

————

... the people of God ought to be the happiest people in all the wide world! People should be coming to us constantly and asking the source of our joy and delight ... [J117]

Heart

God made us for Himself: that is the only explanation that satisfies the *heart* of a thinking man, whatever his wild reason may say. [A33]

————

Keep your heart with all diligence and God will look after the universe. [D67]

————

God is more concerned with the state of people's hearts than with the state of their feelings. [E45]

————

The human heart is heretical by nature. Popular religious beliefs should be checked carefully against the Word of God, for they are almost certain to be wrong. [G98]

Make your heart a vacuum and the Spirit will rush in
to fill it. H41

———

The human heart is heretical by nature and runs to
error as naturally as a garden to weeds. H162

Heaven and Hell

The most godly Christian is the one who knows himself
best, and no one who knows himself will believe that
he deserves anything better than hell.

 The man who knows himself least is likely to have a
cheerful if groundless confidence in his own moral
worth. Such a man has less trouble believing that he
will inherit an eternity of bliss because his concepts are
only quasi-Christian, being influenced strongly by
chimney-corner scripture and old wives' tales. He thinks
of heaven as being very much like California without
the heat and smog, and himself as inhabiting a
splendiferous palace with all modern conveniences, and
wearing a heavily bejeweled crown. Throw in a few
angels and you have the vulgar picture of the future life
held by the devotees of popular Christianity.

 This is the heaven that appears in the saccharin
ballads of the guitar-twanging rockabilly gospellers that
clutter up the religious scene today. That the whole
thing is completely unrealistic and contrary to the laws
of the moral universe seems to make no difference to
anyone. D136

———

The man who is seriously convinced that he deserves to
go to hell is not likely to go there, while the man who

believes that he is worthy of heaven will certainly never enter that blessed place. [H15]

———

Heaven is a place of surrender to the whole will of God and it is heaven because it is such a place. [117]

———

It is safe to say that the pleasurable anticipation of the better things to come has almost died out in the church of Christ. It is a great temptation to take the shallow view that we do not need any heaven promised for tomorrow because we are so well situated here and now. [141]

———

... there is a great company of people all around us needing the reminder that if they are going to go to heaven they had better begin to live like it now and if they expect to die like a Christian they had better live like a Christian now. [142]

———

The corrosive action of unbelief in our day has worn down the Christian hope of heaven until there seems to be very little joy and expectation concerning the eternal inheritance which God has promised. [183]

———

I think we have a right to be startled by the thought that very few people really believe in heaven any more. Oh, we may hear a hillbilly with a guitar singing about heaven in a way that would make an intelligent man turn away from the thought of such a heaven. But, for

the most part, we do not think about heaven very often
and we talk about it even less! [183]

———

I do not see why the idea of relativity or the motions of
the heavenly bodies should destroy or erode the
Christian's faith in heaven as a place. If God could create
an earth and put a race on it, why could He not create
another home and put a redeemed race on it? [185]

History

History is little more than the story of man's sin, and
the daily newspaper a running commentary on it. [D124]

———

When we think of the ebb and flow of man's history
and the inability of men to thwart the reality of death
and judgment, it seems incredible that proud men and
women—both in the church and outside the church—
refuse to give heed to the victorious eternal plan and
program of Jesus Christ! [K150]

Holiness

Go to God and have an understanding. Tell Him that it
is your desire to be holy at any cost and then ask Him
never to give you more happiness than holiness. When
your holiness becomes tarnished, let your joy become
dim. And ask Him to make you holy whether you are
happy or not. Be assured that in the end you will be
as happy as you are holy; but for the time being let your
whole ambition be to serve God and be Christlike. [E46]

God cannot change for the better. Since He is perfectly holy, He has never been less holy than He is now and can never be holier than He is and has always been. Neither can God change for the worse. Any deterioration within the unspeakably holy nature of God is impossible. Indeed I believe it impossible even to think of such a thing, for the moment we attempt to do so, the object about which we are thinking is no longer God but something else and someone less than He. [F55]

———

Holy is the way God is. To be holy He does not conform to a standard. He is that standard. He is absolutely holy with an infinite, incomprehensible fullness of purity that is incapable of being other than it is. Because He is holy, all His attributes are holy; that is, whatever we think of as belonging to God must be thought of as holy. [F112]

———

Every man is as holy as he really wants to be. [H40]

———

. . . although God wants His people to be holy as He is holy, He does not deal with us according to the degree of our holiness but according to the abundance of His mercy. Honesty requires us to admit this. [I55]

———

You cannot study the Bible diligently and earnestly without being struck by an obvious fact—the whole matter of personal holiness is highly important to God! [I59]

Holy Spirit

It is time for us to seek again the leadership of the Holy Ghost. Man's lordship has cost us too much. Man's intrusive will has introduced such a multiplicity of unspiritual ways and unscriptural activities as positively to threaten the life of the Church. These divert annually millions of dollars from the true work of God and waste Christian man-hours in such vast numbers as to be heartbreaking. [B47]

———

The idea of the Spirit held by the average church member is so vague as to be nearly nonexistent. [B66]

———

I think there can be no doubt that the need above all other needs in the Church of God at this moment is the power of the Holy Spirit. More education, better organization, finer equipment, more advanced methods— all are unavailing. It is like bringing a better Pulmotor after the patient is dead. Good as these things are they can never give life. [B92]

———

We may be sure of one thing, that for our deep trouble there is no cure apart from a visitation, yes, an *invasion* of power from above. Only the Spirit Himself can show us what is wrong with us and only the Spirit can prescribe the cure. Only the Spirit can save us from the numbing unreality of Spiritless Christianity. Only the Spirit can show us the Father and the Son. Only the inworking of the Spirit's power can discover to us the solemn majesty and the heart ravishing mystery of the Triune God. [B93]

Before a man can be filled with the Spirit *he must be sure he wants to be.* [B122]

———

Before we can be filled with the Spirit *the desire to be filled must be all-consuming.* It must be for the time the biggest thing in the life, so acute, so intrusive as to crowd out everything else. The degree of fullness in any life accords perfectly with the intensity of true desire. We have as much of God as we actually want. [B124]

———

The Spirit's present work is to honor Him, and everything He does has this for its ultimate purpose. And we must make our thoughts a clean sanctuary for His holy habitation. He dwells in our thoughts, and soiled thoughts are as repugnant to Him as soiled linen to a king. [B125]

———

The inward operation of the Holy Spirit is necessary to saving faith. The gospel is light but only the Spirit can give sight. [D63]

———

The work of the Spirit in the human heart is not an unconscious or automatic thing. Human will and intelligence must yield to and coöperate with the benign intentions of God. [G54]

———

There are two spirits abroad in the earth: the spirit that works in the children of disobedience and the Spirit of God. These two can never be reconciled in time or in eternity. The spirit that dwells in the once-born is forever opposed to the Spirit that inhabits the heart of the twice-born. [H21]

——

Nowhere in the Scriptures nor in Christian biography was anyone ever filled with the Spirit who did not know that he had been, and nowhere was anyone filled who did not know when. And no one was ever filled gradually. [H41]

——

The Holy Spirit is not a luxury meant to make deluxe Christians, as an illuminated frontispiece and a leather binding make a deluxe book. The Spirit is an imperative necessity. Only the Eternal Spirit can do eternal deeds. [H66]

——

. . . many Christians spend a lot of time and energy in making excuses, because they have never broken through into a real offensive for God by the unlimited power of the Holy Spirit! [I34]

——

When the Spirit of God moves into a man's heart, He will make that man generous but He will never make a fool out of him. He will make the man happy but He will never make him silly. He may make him sad with the woe and the weight of the world's grief but He will never let him become a gloomy cynic. The Holy Spirit will make him warmhearted and responsive but He will never cause him to do things of which he will be ashamed later. [I119]

——

. . . the Spirit will make the believing child of God generous but He will never make him foolish! He will make him happy but He will never make him silly! The Spirit will warm the inner life of the Christian's being but He will never lead him to do the same things that would cause him to hang his head in shame afterward. [I129]

———

Many persons preach and teach. Many take part in the music. Certain ones try to administer God's work—but if the power of God's Spirit does not have freedom to energize all they do, these workers might just as well have stayed home. [K12]

———

You can write it down as a fact: no matter what a man does, no matter how successful he seems to be in any field, if the Holy Spirit is not the chief energizer of his activity, it will all fall apart when he dies. [K15]

Idolatry

The essence of idolatry is the entertainment of thoughts about God that are unworthy of Him. [F11]

———

Grace will save a man but it will not save him and his idol. The blood of Christ will shield the penitent sinner alone, but never the sinner and his idol. Faith will justify the sinner, but it will never justify the sinner and his sin. [H90]

Incarnation

In His love and pity God came to us as Christ. [F42]

We know how God would act if He were in our place—
He has been in our place. [G39]

Individuality

... men and women have lost all sight of the fact that
they are important to God. We are all important to God
in setting forth the glory of the Lord Jesus Christ. [J160]

———

... the kingdom of God is not divided into areas for big,
important people and areas for little, unimportant people.
Every one is just as needful in God's sight as any
other! [J161]

———

... one of the supreme glories of man is his many-
sidedness. He can be and do and engage in a variety of
interests and activities. He is not fatally formed to be
only one thing. A rock is formed to be a rock and it
will be a rock until the heavens melt with fervent heat
and the earth passes away. A star is made to shine and
a star it ever will be. The mountain that pushes up into
the sky has been a mountain since the last geological
upheaval pushed it up there. Through all the years it
has worn the garment of force on its back but it has
always been a mountain—never anything else. [J164]

———

When our Lord looked at us, He saw not only what we
were—He was faithful in seeing what we could become!

He took away the curse of being and gave us the glorious blessing of becoming. [J166]

————

Jesus continually placed His emphasis upon the value and worth of the individual. [J168]

————

I find that many men and women are troubled by the thought that they are too small and inconsequential in the scheme of things. But that is not our real trouble—we are actually too big and too complex, for God made us in His image and we are too big to be satisfied with what the world offers us! [J170]

————

Man is bored, because he is too big to be happy with that which sin is giving him. God has made him too great, his potential is too mighty. [J170]

Infinitude

To attribute size to God is to make Him subject to degrees, which He can never be, seeing that the very idea of degree relates to created things only. That which is infinite cannot be greater or less, larger or smaller, and God is infinite. God simply is without qualification. [D72]

————

Infinitude can belong to but One. There can be no second. [F50]

————

Again, to say that God is infinite is to say that He is *measureless*. Measurement is the way created things have of accounting for themselves. It describes limitations, imperfections, and cannot apply to God. Weight describes the gravitational pull of the earth upon material bodies; distance describes intervals between bodies in space; length means extension in space, and there are other familiar measurements such as those for liquid, energy, sound, light, and numbers for pluralities. We also try to measure abstract qualities, and speak of great or little faith, high or low intelligence, large or meager talents.

Is it not plain that all this does not and cannot apply to God? It is the way we see the works of His hands, but not the way we see Him. He is above all this, outside of it, beyond it. [F51]

———

God's gifts in nature have their limitations. They are finite because they have been created, but the gift of eternal life in Christ Jesus is as limitless as God. The Christian man possesses God's own life and shares His infinitude with Him. [F53]

———

God is self-existent and self-contained and knows what no creature can ever know—Himself, perfectly. "*The things of God knoweth no man, but the Spirit of God.*" Only the Infinite can know the infinite. [F63]

———

... the word *infinite* describes what is unique, it can have no modifiers. We do not say "more unique" or "very infinite." Before infinitude we stand silent. [F65]

Influence

Sometimes the best way to see a thing is to look at its opposite. [A105]

There is hardly a man or woman who dares to be just what he or she is without doctoring up the impression. [A114]

——

. . . we fashion ourselves by exposing our lives to the molding influences, good or bad, that lie around us.

> —*Friends.*
> —*Literature.*
> —*Music.*
> —*Pleasures.*
> —*Ambitions.*
> —*Thoughts.*[D128]

——

The things you read will fashion you by slowly conditioning your mind.

The same thing is certainly true of the power of modern films on the minds and morals of those who give themselves over to their influences. [K141]

Knowledge

Knowledge by acquaintance is always better than mere knowledge by description, and the first does not presuppose the second nor require it. [B67]

——

A man can die of starvation knowing all about bread, and a man can remain spiritually dead while knowing all the historic facts of Christianity. [B68]

The philosopher and the scientist will admit that there is much that they do not know; but that is quite another thing from admitting that there is something which they can *never* know, which indeed they have no technique for discovering. F33

———

It is not so important that we know all of the history and all of the scientific facts, but it is vastly important that we desire and know and cherish the Presence of the Living God, who has given Jesus Christ to be the propitiation for our sins; and not for ours only, but also for the sins of the whole world. J17

———

My father was philosophical about many things and I remember that he used to sit during the summertime and ponder why God made the mosquitoes. I still do not have the answer, but I am just a human being, and just because I do not have that answer, I am not going to accuse the Creator of making a cosmic blunder. I know the mosquito is not a blunder—he is just a pest. But God made him.

The same principle is true of a great many other things. I do not know why God does some things, but I am convinced that nothing is accidental in His universe. The fact that we do not know the reason behind some things is not basis enough for us to call them divine accidents. J92

Leadership

Another kind of religious leader must arise among us. He must be of the old prophet type, a man who has seen visions of God and has heard a voice from the Throne. When he comes (and I pray God there will be not one but many) he will stand in flat contradiction to everything our smirking, smooth civilization holds dear. He will contradict, denounce and protest in the name of God and will earn the hatred and opposition of a large segment of Christendom. E23

———

I think the church *has* failed, not by neglecting to provide leadership but by living too much like the world. H138

———

The curse of modern Christian leadership is the pattern of looking around and taking our spiritual bearing from what we see, rather than from what the Lord has said. K65

Life and Death

Only the conquered can know true blessedness. This is sound philosophy, based upon life, and necessary by the constitution of things. We need not accept this truth blindly; the reasons are discoverable, among them being these: We are created beings, and as such are derived, not self-existent. Not to us has it been given to have life in ourselves. For life we are wholly and continually dependent upon God, the Source and Fountain of life. B54

———

Whether we admit it or not the stroke of death is upon us, and it will be saving wisdom for us to learn to trust not in ourselves but in Him that raiseth the dead. B55

To be saved appears to be the highest ambition of most Christians today. To have eternal life and know it is the highest aspiration of many. Here they begin and here they end. C112

———

God offers life, but not an improved old life. The life He offers is life out of death. H44

———

One hundred religious persons knit into a unity by careful organization do not constitute a church any more than eleven dead men make a football team. The first requisite is life, always. H75

———

Back of every wasted life is a bad philosophy, an erroneous conception of life's worth and purpose. H94

Light

If He who called Himself the Light of the World was only a flickering torch, then the darkness that enshrouds the earth is here to stay. B65

———

The only safe light for our path is the light which is reflected from Christ, the Light of the World. C18

———

The man who has met God is not looking for something— he has found it; he is not searching for light—upon him the Light has already shined. C157

To find the way we need more than light; we need also sight. [D59]

Lostness

The man who dies out of Christ is said to be lost, and hardly a word in the English tongue expresses his condition with greater accuracy. He has squandered a rare fortune and at the last he stands for a fleeting moment and looks around, a moral fool, a wastrel who has lost in one overwhelming and irrecoverable loss, his soul, his life, his peace, his total, mysterious personality, his dear and everlasting all. [C99]

——

Men are lost but not abandoned; that is what the Holy Scriptures teach and that is what the Church is commissioned to declare. [D30]

——

The man who does not know where he is is lost; the man who does not know why he was born is worse lost; the man who cannot find an object worthy of his true devotion is lost utterly; and by this description the human race is lost, and it is a part of our lostness that we do not know how lost we are. [H93]

——

I hope that God can burn this frightful fact into our souls—the truth that men and women can be respectable and religious and prayerful and careful and eager and ask the right questions and talk about religion—and still be lost! J55

Love

The gravest question any of us face is whether we do or do not love the Lord. G132

———

. . . the final test of love is obedience. Not sweet emotions, not willingness to sacrifice, not zeal, but obedience to the commandments of Christ. G134

———

Love for Christ is a love of willing as well as a love of feeling, and it is psychologically impossible to love Him adequately unless we will to obey His words. G134

———

No law has ever been passed that can compel one moral being to love another, for by the very nature of it love must be voluntary. No one can be coerced or frightened into loving anyone. H35

Man

Everyone of us has had experiences which we have not been able to explain: a sudden sense of loneliness, or a feeling of wonder or awe in the face of the universal vastness. Or we have had a fleeting visitation of light like an illumination from some other sun, giving us in a quick flash an assurance that we are from another world, that our origins are divine. A78

The burden borne by mankind is a heavy and a crushing thing. [A111]

———

We must never underestimate the ability of human beings to get themselves tangled up. [C83]

———

One thing seems to be quite forgotten: the world moves and times change but people remain the same always. [C155]

———

A man is the sum of his parts and his character the sum of the traits that compose it. [F22]

———

Because man is born a rebel, he is unaware that he is one. His constant assertion of self, as far as he thinks of it at all, appears to him a perfectly normal thing. He is willing to share himself, sometimes even to sacrifice himself for a desired end, but never to dethrone himself. [F36]

———

We have but to become acquainted with, or even listen to, the big names of our times to discover how wretchedly inferior most of them are. Many appear to have arrived at their present eminence by pull, brass, nerve, gall and lucky accident. We turn away from them sick to our stomach and wonder for a discouraged moment if this is the best the human race can produce. [H96]

The teaching of the New Testament is that now, at this very moment, there is a man in heaven appearing in the presence of God for us. He is as certainly a man as was Adam or Moses or Paul. He is a man glorified, but His glorification did not dehumanize Him. Today He is a real man, of the race of mankind, bearing our lineaments and dimensions, a visible and audible man whom any other man would recognize instantly as one of us. [H142]

———

It is now quite possible to talk for hours with civilized men and women and gain absolutely nothing from it. Conversation today is almost wholly sterile. Should the talk start on a fairly high level, it is sure within a few minutes to degenerate into cheap gossip, shoptalk, banter, weak humor, stale jokes, puns and secondhand quips. [H144]

———

The modern civilized man is impatient; he takes the short-range view of things. He is surrounded by gadgets that get things done in a hurry. He was brought up on quick oats; he likes his instant coffee; he wears drip-dry shirts and takes one-minute Polaroid snapshots of his children. His wife shops for her spring hat before the leaves are down in the fall. His new car, if he buys it after June 1, is already an old model when he brings it home. He is almost always in a hurry and can't bear to wait for anything.

This breathless way of living naturally makes for a mentality impatient of delay, and when this man enters the kingdom of God he brings his short-range psychology with him. He finds prophecy too slow for him. [H155]

126

The faith of Christ offers no buttons to push for quick service. The new order must wait the Lord's own time, and that is too much for the man in a hurry. He just gives up and becomes interested in something else. [H156]

———

. . . it is characteristic of the natural man to keep himself so busy with unimportant trifles that he is able to avoid the settling of the most important matters relating to life and existence. [J10]

Fall of Man

The fall of man has created a perpetual crisis. It will last until sin has been put down and Christ reigns over a redeemed and restored world. [D28]

———

. . . the Fall was a moral crisis but it has affected every part of man's nature, moral, intellectual, psychological, spiritual and physical. His whole being has been deeply injured; the sin in his heart has overflowed into his total life, affecting his relation to God, to his fellow men and to everyone and everything that touches him. [D29]

———

It is an ironic thought . . . that fallen men, though they cannot fulfill their promises, are always able to make good on their threats. For decades they have been promising us a warless world where peace and brotherhood shall sit quiet as a brooding dove. All they have given us is the control of a few diseases and the debilitating comforts of push-button living. These have extended our lives a little longer so we are now able to stay around to see our generation die one by one; and when the riper years come upon us they retire us by compulsion and turn us out to clutter up a world that has no place for us, a world that does not understand us and that we do not understand. D110

Inner Man

... *being* has ceased to have much appeal for people and *doing* engages almost everyone's attention. Modern Christians lack symmetry. They know almost nothing about the inner life. C75

———

Deep inside every man there is a private sanctum where dwells the mysterious essence of his being. H9

———

There is a sense in which our bodies actually veil us from one another. We are uncertain. We shake a hand and look at a face. The influence of that hand or face is a physical thing—and the real you, the inner man, is deeper than that, and beyond and past all of that. J35

———

... Jesus came in order that our spirits might prosper! He came that our inner man, the eternal and undying part of us, might prosper! J36

Mind

Whatever men may think of human reason God takes a low view of it. [B78]

———

The difficulty we modern Christians face is not misunderstanding the Bible, but persuading our untamed hearts to accept its plain instructions. Our problem is to get the consent of our world-loving minds to make Jesus Lord in fact as well as in word. [B114]

———

Evangelicals at the moment appear to be divided into two camps—those who trust the human intellect to the point of sheer rationalism, and those who are shy of everything intellectual and are convinced that thinking is a waste of the Christian's time.

Surely both are wrong. Self-conscious intellectualism is offensive to man and, I am convinced, to God also but it is significant that every major revelation in the Scriptures was made to a man of superior intellect. It would be easy to marshall an imposing list of Biblical quotations exhorting us to think, but a more convincing argument is the whole drift of the Bible itself. The Scriptures simply take for granted that the saints of the Most High will be serious-minded, thoughtful persons. They never leave the impression that it is sinful to think. [G52]

———

. . . a guileless mind is a great treasure; it is worth any price. [H91]

Our intellectual activities in the order of their importance may be graded this way: first, cogitation; second, observation; third, reading. [H144]

———

... pure thinking will do more to educate a man than any other activity he can engage in. To afford sympathetic entertainment to abstract ideas, to let one idea beget another, and that another, till the mind teems with them; to compare one idea with others, to weigh, to consider, evaluate, approve, reject, correct, refine; to join thought with thought like an architect till a noble edifice has been created within the mind; to travel back in imagination to the beginning of the creation and then to leap swiftly forward to the end of time; to bound upward through illimitable space and downward into the nucleus of an atom; and all this without so much as moving from our chair or opening the eyes—this is to soar above all the lower creation and to come near to the angels of God. [H145]

———

Knowledge is the raw material out of which that finest of all machines, the mind, creates its amazing world. [H146]

———

Perception of ideas rather than the storing of them should be the aim of education. The mind should be an eye to see with rather than a bin to store facts in. The man who has been taught by the Holy Spirit will be a seer rather than a scholar. The difference is that the scholar sees and the seer sees through; and that is a mighty difference indeed. [H150]

——

The human intellect even in its fallen state is an awesome work of God, but it lies in darkness until it has been illuminated by the Holy Spirit. Our Lord has little good to say of the unilluminated mind, but He revels in the mind that has been renewed and enlightened by grace. He always makes the place of His feet glorious; there is scarcely anything on earth more beautiful than a Spirit-filled mind, certainly nothing more wonderful than an alert and eager mind made incandescent by the presence of the indwelling Christ. [H150]

——

Much of the religious activity we see in the churches is not the eternal working of the Eternal Spirit, but the mortal working of man's mortal mind—and that is raw tragedy!

From what I see and sense in evangelical circles, I would have to say that about ninety per cent of the religious work carried on in the churches is being done by ungifted members. [K33]

——

Talented people everywhere think that their feet or their hands, their ears or their vocal chords are the means of their productions.

There never was a greater mistake than to believe that!

The credit all has to go to the marvelous brain that God has given every man. The hands have never really done anything except at the bidding and control of the brain.

If the brain should suddenly be cut off and die, the hands will lie limp and helpless. It is the brain of a man that paints a picture, smells a rose, hears the sound of music. [K37]

Money

... the very smell of the currency we pass around indicates where it has been. It smells of itself—as though it could tell its own story of crime and violence and immorality! [B90]

Morality

... the cause of all our human miseries is a radical dislocation, an upset in our relation to God and to each other. [A99]

The moral state of the penitent when he comes to Christ does not affect the result, for the work of Christ sweeps away both his good and his evil and turns him into another man. [B27]

Within the last century man has leaped ahead in scientific achievement but has lagged behind morally, with the result that he is now technically capable of destroying the world and morally incapable of restraining himself from doing so. [E29]

The New Testament knows nothing of the working of the Spirit in us apart from our own moral responses. [G54]

132

Moral power has always accompanied definitive beliefs. Great saints have always been dogmatic. We need right now a return to a gentle dogmatism that smiles while it stands stubborn and firm on the Word of God that liveth and abideth forever. [H164]

Mortality and Immortality

It is God Almighty who puts eternity in a man's breast and tomorrow in a man's heart and gives His people immortality, so what you see down here really is not much. But when the bird of immortality takes to the wing, she sails on and on, over the horizon and out into the everlasting tomorrows and never comes down and never dies. [J83]

———

. . . mortality is the sentence of death. Death is the carrying out of the sentence of mortality. They are not the same. Death is the final act—man's mortality lies in his knowledge that he can never escape! [J107]

Motive

The man of God set his heart to exalt God above all; God accepted his intention as fact and acted accordingly. Not perfection, but holy intention made the difference. [A106]

———

The "layman" need never think of his humbler task as being inferior to that of his minister. Let every man

abide in the calling wherein he is called and his work
will be as sacred as the work of the ministry. It is not
what a man does that determines whether his work
is sacred or secular, it is *why* he does it. The motive is
everything. Let a man sanctify the Lord God in his heart
and he can thereafter do no common act. All he does is
good and acceptable to God through Jesus Christ. For
such a man, living itself will be sacramental and the
whole world a sanctuary. [A127]

—

The test by which all conduct must finally be judged is
motive.

As water cannot rise higher than its source, so the
moral quality in an act can never be higher than the
motive that inspires it. [C89]

—

Religious acts done out of low motives are twice evil,
evil in themselves and evil because they are done in the
name of God. [C90]

—

Christians, and especially very active ones, should take
time out frequently to search their souls to be sure of
their motives. Many a solo is sung to show off; many a
sermon is preached as an exhibition of talent; many a
church is founded as a slap at some other church. Even
missionary activity may become competitive, and soul
winning may degenerate into a sort of brush-salesman
project to satisfy the flesh. Do not forget, the Pharisees
were great missionaries and would compass sea and
land to make a convert. [C90]

Music

If you give yourself to the contemporary fare of music
that touches the baser emotions, it will shape your mind
and emotions and desires, whether you admit it or not. [K142]

New Birth

A Christian is what he is not by ecclesiastical
manipulation but by the new birth. He is a Christian
because of a Spirit which dwells in him. [B111]

———

. . . men do not become Christians by associating with
church people, nor by religious contact, nor by religious
education; they become Christians only by an invasion
of their nature by the Spirit of God in the New Birth. [B113]

———

The new birth makes us partakers of the divine nature.
There the work of undoing the dissimilarity between us
and God beings. [D122]

———

The genuinely renewed man will have a new life center.
He will experience a new orientation affecting his whole
personality. He will become aware of a different
philosophic outlook. Things he once held to be of value
may suddenly lose all their attraction for him and he
may even hate some things he formerly loved.

The man who recoils from this revolutionary kind of
Christianity is retreating before the cross. But thousands
do so retreat, and they try to make things right by

seeking baptism and church membership. No wonder
they are so dissatisfied. [H63]

———

Whoever is born of God is one with everyone else who
is born of God. Just as gold is always gold, wherever
and in whatever shape it is found, and every detached
scrap of gold belongs to the true family and is composed
of the same element, so every regenerate soul belongs
to the universal Christian community and to the
fellowship of the saints. [H74]

———

If we believe the New Testament we must surely believe
that the new birth is a major miracle, as truly a miracle
of God as was the first creation, for the new birth is
actually the creating of another man in the heart where
another man had been. [137]

———

. . . to be genuinely born again is the miracle of becoming
a partaker of the divine nature. It is more than just a
religious expression; more than the hyphenated adjective
we often hear, such as "He's a born-again man." [139]

———

. . . there are many who talk about being born again on
the basis of their mental assent to Christian principles.
I think there are many who have received Christ mentally
who have never discoverd the supernatural quality of
the grace of God or of the acts of God. [139]

Obedience

Obedience to the word of Christ will bring an inward
revelation of the Godhead. [A58]

God being who He is must have obedience from His creatures. Man being who he is must render that obedience. C143

——

. . . the Christian can hope for no manifestation of God while he lives in a state of disobedience. Let a man refuse to obey God on some clear point, let him set his will stubbornly to resist any commandment of Christ, and the rest of his religious activities will be wasted. He may go to church for fifty years to no profit. He may tithe, teach, preach, sing, write or edit or run a Bible conference till he gets too old to navigate and have nothing but ashes at the last. *"To obey is better than sacrifice."* D102

——

The exhortations in the epistles are to be understood as apostolic injunctions carrying the weight of mandatory charges from the Head of the Church. They are intended to be obeyed, not weighed as bits of good advice which we are at liberty to accept or reject as we will. E53

——

If we would have God's blessing upon us we must begin to obey. Prayer will become effective when we stop using it as a substitute for obedience. God will not accept praying in lieu of obeying. We only deceive ourselves when we try to make the substitution. E53

——

We must be willing to obey if we would know the true inner meaning of the teachings of Christ and the apostles. G93

"If any man love the world, the love of the Father is not in him." This requires no comment, only obedience. [H65]

———

... obedience is taught throughout the entire Bible ... true obedience is one of the toughest requirements of the Christian life. Apart from obedience, there can be no salvation, for salvation without obedience is a self-contradictory impossibility. [I11]

———

The life of obedience to Jesus Christ means living moment by moment in the Spirit of God and it will be so different from your former life that you will often be considered strange. In fact, the life in the Spirit is such a different life that some of your former associates will probably discuss the question of whether or not you are mentally disturbed. The true Christian may seem a strange person indeed to those who make their observations only from the point of view of this present world which is alienated from God and His gracious plan of salvation. [I139]

Old and New

Nothing that matters is new. [D88]

———

Nothing is new that matters and nothing that matters can be modernized. [D88]

Nothing new can save my soul; neither can saving grace be modernized. We must each come as Abel came, by atoning blood and faith demonstrated in repentance. No new way has been discovered. The old way is the true way and there is no new way. The Lamb of God was slain *"before the foundation of the world."* D90

Optimism and Pessimism

The cross-carrying Christian . . . is both a confirmed pessimist and an optimist the like of which is to be found nowhere else on earth. G13

——

Strange as it may be, the holiest souls who have ever lived have earned the reputation for being pessimistic. H98

——

No, the unknown saints are not pessimists, nor are they misanthropes or joy-killers. They are by virtue of their godly faith the world's only true optimists. H98

Peace

What wicked men do should not disturb the good man's tranquillity. D65

——

True peace is a gift of God and today it is found only in the minds of innocent children and in the hearts of trustful Christians. D110

It is time that we Christians awake to the fact that the world cannot help us in anything that matters. Not the educators nor the legislators nor the scientists can bring us tranquillity of heart, and without tranquillity whatever else they give us is useless at last. [D110]

———

The knowledge that we are never alone calms the troubled sea of our lives and speaks peace to our souls. [F82]

———

It appears that most people go to church for consolation. In fact, we have now fallen upon times when religion is mostly for consolation. We are now in the grip of the cult of peace—peace of mind, peace of heart, peace of soul, and we want to relax and have the great God Almighty pat our heads and comfort us. This has become religion. [J19]

Personality

A loving Personality dominates the Bible, walking among the trees of the garden and breathing fragrance over every scene. Always a living Person is present, speaking, pleading, loving, working, and manifesting Himself whenever and wherever His people have the receptivity necessary to receive the manifestation. [A50]

———

He can invade the human heart and make room for Himself without expelling anything essentially human.

The integrity of the human personality remains
unimpaired. [B69]

———

Human personality is dear to God because it is of all
created things the nearest to being like Himself. [C98]

———

A good personality and a shrewd knowledge of human
nature is all that any man needs to be a success in
religious circles today. [D59]

———

In this day when shimmering personalities carry on the
Lord's work after the methods of the entertainment
world it is refreshing to associate for a moment even in
the pages of a book with a sincere and humble man
who keeps his own personality out of sight and places
the emphasis upon the inworking of God. [E18]

Possession

The man who has God for his treasure has all things in
One. Many ordinary treasures may be denied him, or
if he is allowed to have them, the enjoyment of them
will be so tempered that they will never be necessary to
his happiness. Or if he must see them go, one after
one, he will scarcely feel a sense of loss, for having the
Source of all things he has in One all satisfaction, all
pleasure, all delight. Whatever he may lose he has actually
lost nothing, for he now has it all in One, and he has it
purely, legitimately and forever. [A20]

The way to deeper knowledge of God is through the lonely valleys of soul poverty and abnegation of all things. The blessed ones who possess the Kingdom are they who have repudiated every external thing and have rooted from their hearts all sense of possessing. [A23]

———

These blessed poor are no longer slaves to the tyranny of *things*. They have broken the yoke of the oppressor; and this they have done not by fighting but by surrendering. Though free from all sense of possessing, they yet possess all things. [A23]

———

In the kingdom of God the surest way to lose something is to try to protect it, and the best way to keep it is to let it go. [D96]

———

A real Christian need not defend his possession nor his position. God will take care of both. Let go of your treasures and the Lord will keep them for you unto life eternal. Hang onto them and they will bring you nothing but trouble and misery to the end of your days. [D99]

———

Any temporal possession can be turned into everlasting wealth. Whatever is given to Christ is immediately touched with immortality. [D107]

Prayer

Prayer at its best is the expression of the total life. [C81]

All things else being equal, our prayers are only as powerful as our lives. In the long pull we pray only as well as we live. [C81]

———

As we go on into God we shall see the excellency of the life of constant communion where all thoughts and acts are prayers, and the entire life becomes one holy sacrifice of praise and worship. [C82]

———

The average service in gospel circles these days is kept alive by noise. By making a lot of religious din we assure our faltering hearts that everything is well and, conversely, we suspect silence and regard it as a proof that the meeting is "dead." Even the most devout seem to think they must storm heaven with loud outcries and mighty bellowings or their prayers are of no avail. [C145]

———

We pour out millions of words and never notice that the prayers are not answered. [D34]

———

. . . we not only do not expect our prayers to be answered but would be embarrassed or even disappointed if they were. I think it is not uncommon for Christians to present eloquent petitions to the Lord which they know will accomplish nothing, and some of those petitions they dare present only because they know that is the last they will hear of the whole thing. Many a wordy

brother would withdraw his request quickly enough if
he had any intimation that God was taking it seriously. [D34]

... there are some things that not even prayer can
change. [D66]

When we become too glib in prayer we are most surely
talking to ourselves. [D87]

In the average church we hear the same prayers repeated
each Sunday year in and year out with, one would
suspect, not the remotest expectation that they will be
answered. It is enough, it seems, that they have been
uttered. The familiar phrase, the religious tone, the
emotionally loaded words have their superficial and
temporary effect, but the worshiper is no nearer to God,
no better morally and no surer of heaven than he was
before. [D100]

In our private prayers and in our public services we are
forever asking God to do things that He either has
already done or cannot do because of our unbelief. We
plead for Him to speak when He has already spoken
and is at that very moment speaking. We ask Him to
come when He is already present and waiting for us to
recognize Him. We beg the Holy Spirit to fill us while
all the time we are preventing Him by our doubts. [D102]

Piqued prayers can be dangerous. [E93]

Retire from the world each day to some private spot,
even if it be only the bedroom (for a while I retreated to
the furnace room for want of a better place). Stay in
the secret place till the surrounding noises begin to fade
out of your heart and a sense of God's presence envelops
you. Deliberately tune out the unpleasant sounds and
come out of your closet determined not to hear them.
Listen for the inward Voice till you learn to recognize
it. Stop trying to compete with others. Give yourself
to God and then be what and who you are without regard
to what others think. Reduce your interests to a few.
Don't try to know what will be of no service to you.
Avoid the digest type of mind—short bits or unrelated
facts, cute stories and bright sayings. Learn to pray
inwardly every moment. After a while you can do this
even while you work. Practice candor, childlike honesty,
humility. Pray for a single eye. Read less, but read more
of what is important to your inner life. Never let your
mind remain scattered for very long. Call home your
roving thoughts. Gaze on Christ with the eyes of your
soul. Practice spiritual concentration.

All the above is contingent upon a right relation to
God through Christ and daily meditation on the
Scriptures. Lacking these, nothing will help us; granted
these, the discipline recommended will go far to
neutralize the evil effects of externalism and to make
us acquainted with God and our own souls. E106

———

When we are praying for something we have every right
to look for the answer. Never should we fear to look at
the facts. Either God answered or He did not, and there
is no point in shutting our eyes and refusing to admit
it when it is plain that no answer has been received. It

may be that we shall need to trust Him without an answer and hold on quietly in prayer when our case looks hopeless. But we cannot help things by claiming He has answered when He has not. E123

———

Prayer is not in itself meritorious. It lays God under no obligation nor puts Him in debt to any. He hears prayer because He is good, and for no other reason. Nor is faith meritorious; it is simply confidence in the goodness of God, and the lack of it is a reflection upon God's holy character. F89

———

Prayer is not a sure fire protection against error for the reason that there are many kinds of prayer and some of them are worse than useless. G50

———

In spite of the difficulties we encounter when we pray, prayer is a powerful and effective way to get right, stay right and stay free from error. G51

———

It is futile to beg God to act contrary to His revealed purposes. To pray with confidence the petitioner must be certain that his request falls within the broad will of God for His people H86

———

A man may engage in a great deal of humble talk before God and get no response because unknown to himself he is using prayer to disguise disobedience. H90

When Peter was starting to sink under those waters of Galilee, he had no time to consult the margin of someone's Bible to find out how he should pray. He just prayed out of his heart and out of his desperation, "Lord, save me!" [J103]

———

If a man will just get his heart down on its knees, he will find that there is an awful lot that he does not need to know to receive Jesus Christ! [J103]

Preaching

To speak to God on behalf of men is probably the highest service any of us can render. The next is to speak to men in the name of God. Either is a privilege possible to us only through the grace of our Lord Jesus Christ. [D1]

———

We who preach the gospel must not think of ourselves as public relations agents sent to establish good will between Christ and the world. We must not imagine ourselves commissioned to make Christ acceptable to big business, the press, the world of sports or modern education. We are not diplomats but prophets, and our message is not a compromise but an ultimatum. [H44]

———

In a very real sense no man can teach another; he can only aid him to teach himself. [H149]

... we need to preach again a whole Christ to the world—a Christ who does not need our apologies, a Christ who will not be divided, a Christ who will either be Lord of all or who will not be Lord at all! [115]

———

I feel sorry for the church that decides to call a man to the pulpit because "his personality simply sparkles!" [K41]

Progress

Progress in the Christian life is exactly equal to the growing knowledge we gain of the Triune God in personal experience. [C11]

———

At the risk of being written off as an extremist or a borderline fanatic we offer it as our mature opinion that more spiritual progress can be made in one short moment of speechless silence in the awesome presence of God than in years of mere study. [C146]

———

No responsible person will deny that some changes made by the race over the years have been improvements, and so may have represented progress and advance, though just what we are supposed to be advancing toward has not been made very clear by our leaders. And it would seem to be difficult to show that we are moving toward an end when we do not know what or where that end is, or even if such an end exists at all. [C155]

Prophets

Between the scribe who has read and the prophet who has seen there is a difference as wide as the sea. We are today overrun with orthodox scribes, but the prophets, where are they? The hard voice of the scribe sounds over evangelicalism, but the Church waits for the tender voice of the saint who has penetrated the veil and has gazed with inward eye upon the Wonder that is God. [A43]

———

A prophet is one who knows his times and what God is trying to say to the people of his times. [E20]

———

Scholars can interpret the past; it takes prophets to interpret the present. [E22]

———

Much of the Bible is devoted to prediction. Nothing God has yet done for us can compare with all that is written in the sure word of prophecy. And nothing He has done or may yet do for us can compare with *what He is and will be to us.* [E126]

———

The New Testament gift of prophecy was not to predict— but to tell forth what God has to say and to proclaim God's truth for the present age. [K25]

Protestantism

Protestantism is on the wrong road when it tries to win merely by means of a "united front." It is not organizational unity we need most; the great need is power. The headstones in the cemetery present a united front, but they stand mute and helpless while the world passes by. [B92]

———

The casual indifference with which millions of Protestants view their God-blessed religious liberty is ominous. Being let go they go on weekends to the lakes and mountains and beaches to play shuffleboard, fish and sun bathe. They go where their heart is and come back to the praying company only when the bad weather drives them in. Let this continue long enough and evangelical Protestantism will be ripe for a take-over by Rome. [H160]

———

It is a generally accepted fact that most Protestant Christians serve the Lord at their own convenience. We say we believe in such things as prayer and fasting but we do not practice them unless it is convenient. Very few of us are willing to get up before daybreak as many Catholics do in order to be present in their daily services.

I am not saying that we ought to be Catholics, but I am saying that we have great throngs of professing Christians who are the slickest bunch alive in getting their religion for nothing! [J71]

Redemption

The whole purpose of God in redemption is to make us holy and to restore us to the image of God. To accomplish this He disengages us from earthly ambitions and draws us away from the cheap and unworthy prizes that worldly men set their hearts upon. [C25]

——

The first announcement of God's redemptive intention toward mankind was made to a man and a woman hiding in mortal fear from the presence of the Lord. [C38]

——

The primary work of Christ in redemption is to justify, sanctify and ultimately to glorify a company of persons salvaged from the ruin of the human race. [D139]

——

Surely this is not the time for pale faces and trembling knees among the sons of the new creation. The darker the night the brighter faith shines and the sooner comes the morning. Look up and lift up your heads; our redemption draweth near. [E132]

——

For human beings the whole possibility of redemption lies in their ability to change. [F57]

——

The purpose of Christ's redeeming work was to make it possible for bad men to become good—deeply, radically and finally. [H64]

——

Every redeemed soul is born out of the same spiritual life as every other redeemed soul and partakes of the divine nature in exactly the same manner. [H75]

The purpose and work of redemption in Christ Jesus is to raise man as much above the level of Adam as Christ Himself is above the level of Adam. We are to gaze upon Christ, not Adam, and in so doing are being transformed by the Spirit of God into Christ's image. [J:14]

Regeneration

In the Bible the offer of pardon on the part of God is conditioned upon intention to reform on the part of man. There can be no spiritual regeneration till there has been a moral reformation. [C42]

The converted man is both reformed and regenerated. And unless the sinner is willing to reform his way of living he will never know the inward experience of regeneration. [C43]

Man's hopeless condition cannot be perfected by some slow process of social regeneration—it must be brought about through the miraculous process of individual regeneration. [J168]

Regret

Regret may be no more than a form of self-love. A man may have such a high regard for himself that any failure to live up to his own image of himself disappoints him deeply. He feels that he has betrayed his better self by his act of wrongdoing, and even if God is willing to forgive him he will not forgive himself. Sin brings to such a man a painful loss of face that is not soon forgotten. He becomes permanently angry with himself and tries to punish himself by going to God frequently with petulant self-accusations. This state of mind crystallizes finally into a feeling of chronic regret which appears to be a proof of deep penitence but is actually proof of deep self-love. [G100]

———

Regret for a sinful past will remain until we truly believe that for us in Christ that sinful past no longer exists. The man in Christ has only Christ's past and that is perfect and acceptable to God. In Christ he died, in Christ he rose, and in Christ he is seated within the circle of God's favored ones. He is no longer angry with himself because he is no longer self-regarding, but Christ-regarding; hence there is no place for regret. [G100]

Religion

Religion, so far as it is genuine, is in essence the response of created personalities to the Creating Personality, God. *"This is life eternal, that they might know thee the only true God, and Jesus Christ, whom thou hast sent."* [A13]

———

I have not said that religion without power makes no changes in a man's life, only that it makes no fundamental difference. Water may change from liquid to vapor, from vapor to snow and back to liquid again, and still be fundamentally the same. So powerless religion may put a man through many surface changes and leave him exactly what he was before. [B33]

Religious extroversion has been carried to such an extreme in evangelical circles that hardly anyone has the desire, to say nothing of the courage, to question the soundness of it. Externalism has taken over. C75

———

The pitiable attempt of churchmen to explain everything for the smiling unbeliever has had an effect exactly opposite to that which was intended. It has reduced worship to the level of the intellect and introduced the rationalistic spirit into the wonders of religion. C79

———

. . . religion is disengaged from practical life and retired to the airy region of fancy where dwell the sweet insubstantial nothings which everyone knows do not exist but which they nevertheless lack the courage to repudiate publicly.

I could wish that this were true only of pagan religions and of the vague and ill-defined quasi-religion of the average man; but candor dictates that I admit it to be true also of much that passes for evangelical Christianity in our times. Indeed it is more than possible that the gods of the heathen are more real to them than is the God of the average Christian. D33

———

We settle for words in religion because deeds are too costly. It is easier to pray, "Lord, help me to carry my cross daily" than to pick up the cross and carry it; but since the mere request for help to do something we do not actually intend to do has a certain degree of religious comfort, we are content with repetition of the words. D34

When Christ came with His blazing spiritual penetration and His fine moral sensitivity He appeared to the Pharisee to be a devotee of another kind of religion, which indeed He was if the world had only understood. [D94]

With Bibles under their arms and bundles of tracts in their pockets, religious persons now meet to carry on "services" so carnal, so pagan, that they can hardly be distinguished from the old vaudeville shows of earlier days. And for a preacher or a writer to challenge this heresy is to invite ridicule and abuse from every quarter. [E19]

The essence of true religion is spontaneity, the sovereign movings of the Holy Spirit upon and in the free spirit of redeemed man. [E70]

When religion loses its sovereign character and becomes mere form this spontaneity is lost also, and in its place come precedent, propriety, system—and the file-card mentality. [E70]

. . . no religion has ever been greater than its idea of God. Worship is pure or base as the worshiper entertains high or low thoughts of God. [F9]

True religion is removed from diet and days, from garments and ceremonies, and placed where it belongs—in the union of the spirit of man with the Spirit of God. [H10]

Our Lord knew that in these times there would be those in our churches who are just highly-groomed show-pieces of Christianity—middle class and well-to-do, satisfied with a religious life that costs them nothing. L70

——

In this dim world of pious sentiment all religions are equal and any man who insists that salvation is by Jesus Christ alone is a bigot and a boor.

So we pool our religious light, which if the truth is told is little more than darkness visible; we discuss religion on television and in the press as a kind of game, much as we discuss art and philosophy, accepting as one of the ground rules of the game that there is no final test of truth and that the best religion is a composite of the best in all religions. H113

——

One mark of the low state of affairs among us is religious boredom. H134

——

We are paying a frightful price for our religious boredom. And that at the moment of the world's mortal peril. H136

——

. . . the only two motives that remain in the wide world for religion. If you are not good, they warn, civilization will fall apart and the bomb will get us all, and if you do not come to the Lord, you will never have peace!

So, between fear and the desire to be patted and chucked under the chin and cuddled, the professing Christian staggers along his way. J19

Man's great difficulty is that we have religion without guilt, and religion without guilt just tries to make God a big "pal" of man. [J36]

———

Religion without any consciousness of guilt is a false religion. [J37]

———

Most of the shallow psychology religions of the day try to deal with the problem of the ego by jockeying it around from one position to another, but Christianity deals with the problem of *I* by disposing of it with finality. [J122]

Repentance

I think there is little doubt that the teaching of salvation without repentance has lowered the moral standards of the Church and produced a multitude of deceived religious professors who erroneously believe themselves to be saved when in fact they are still in the gall of bitterness and the bond of iniquity. [C44]

———

God will take nine steps toward us, but He will not take the tenth. He will *incline* us to repent, but He cannot do our repenting for us. [G30]

Reproof

When reproved pay no attention to the source. Do not ask whether it is a friend or an enemy that reproves

you. An enemy is often of greater value to you than a
friend because he is not influenced by sympathy. C30

——

Keep your heart open to the correction of the Lord and
be ready to receive His chastisement regardless of who
holds the whip. C30

Resurrection

If men do not rise again from the dead, then we are of
all men most miserable—and that is still the truth!
    The promise of the resurrection makes the difference
for the man who is a believing Christian. If men are not
to be raised from the dead, why not eat, drink and be
merry, for tomorrow we die! J82

——

The Christian church is helpless and hopeless if it is
stripped of the reality and historicity of the bodily
resurrection of Jesus Christ. K100

Revival

It is easy to learn the doctrine of personal revival and
victorious living; it is quite another thing to take our
cross and plod on to the dark and bitter hill of self-
renunciation. D9

——

. . . all of us who love our Lord Jesus Christ are facing
such great changes in this period before the return of
Christ that we are going to have to recall and have back
upon us the kind of spiritual revival that will eventuate

in a new moral power, in a new spirit of willing separation and heart purity, and a new bestowing of the enablings of the Spirit of God. K67

Righteousness

It appears that too many Christians want to enjoy the thrill of feeling right but are not willing to endure the inconvenience of being right. C52

———

There are areas in our lives where in our effort to be right we may go wrong, so wrong as to lead to spiritual deformity. To be specific let me name a few:

1. *When in our determination to be bold we become brazen.*
2. *When in our desire to be frank we become rude.*
3. *When in our effort to be watchful we become suspicious.*
4. *When we seek to be serious and become somber.*
5. *When we mean to be conscientious and become overscrupulous.* G54

———

When God *declares* a man righteous He instantly sets about to *make* him righteous. Our error today is that we do not expect a converted man to be a transformed man, and as a result of this error our churches are full of substandard Christians. H65

———

To be right with God has often meant to be in trouble with men. H114

Sainthood

However deep the mystery, however many the paradoxes involved, it is still true that men become saints not at their own whim but by sovereign calling. [B48]

——

Occasionally one's heart is cheered by the discovery of some insatiable saint who is willing to sacrifice everything for the sheer joy of experiencing God in increasing intimacy. To such we offer this word of exhortation: Pray on, fight on, sing on. Do not underrate anything God may have done for you heretofore. Thank God for everything up to this point, but do not stop here. Press on into the deep things of God. Insist upon tasting the profounder mysteries of redemption. Keep your feet on the ground, but let your heart soar as high as it will. Refuse to be average or to surrender to the chill of your spiritual environment. [C56]

——

The average so-called Bible Christian in our times is but a wretched parody on true sainthood. [E13]

——

We must insist on new Testament sainthood for our converts, nothing less; and we must lead them into a state of heart purity, fiery love, separation from the world and poured-out devotion to the Person of Christ. [E13]

——

There is a sense in which God makes no difference between the saint and the sinner. He maketh His sun to rise on the evil and on the good, and sendeth rain on the just and on the unjust. It is strange that we rarely

notice the other side of this truth: that God also visits
His children with the usual problems common to all
the sons of men. The Christian will feel the heat on a
sweltering day; the cold will bite into his skin as certainly
as into that of his unsaved neighbor; he will be affected
by war and peace, booms and depressions, without regard
to his spiritual state. To believe otherwise is to go
beyond the Scriptures and to falsify the experience of
the saints in every age. [E101]

Salvation

Essentially salvation is the restoration of a right relation
between man and his Creator, a bringing back to normal
of the Creator-creature relation. [A99]

_____

Salvation must include a judicial change of status, but
what is overlooked by most teachers is that *it also
includes an actual change in the life of the individual.*
And by this we mean more than a surface change, we
mean a transformation as deep as the roots of his human
life. [B37]

_____

Salvation is from our side a choice, from the divine side
it is a seizing upon, an apprehending, a conquest by
the Most High God. *Our "accepting" and "willing" are
reactions rather than actions.* The right of
determination must always remain with God. [B49]

_____

We might well pray for God to invade and conquer us,
for until He does, we remain in peril from a thousand

foes. We bear within us the seeds of our own disintegration. Our moral imprudence puts us always in danger of accidental or reckless self-destruction. The strength of our flesh is an ever present danger to our souls. Deliverance can come to us only by the defeat of our old life. Safety and peace come only after we have been forced to our knees. God rescues us by breaking us, by shattering our strength and wiping out our resistance. Then He invades our natures with that ancient and eternal life which is from the beginning. So He conquers us and by that benign conquest saves us for Himself. B57

———

They who follow a merely human Saviour follow no Saviour at all, but an ideal only, and one furthermore that can do no more than mock their weaknesses and sins. B64

———

It is altogether doubtful whether any man can be saved who comes to Christ for His help but with no intention to obey Him. C85

———

... the whole modern notion embodied in our common phrase "soul winning" could stand a good overhauling in the light of the broader teachings of the Scriptures. C97

———

For a long generation we have been holding the letter of truth while at the same time we have been moving away from it in spirit because we have been preoccupied with what we are saved *from* rather than what we have been saved *to*. G44

Evangelical Christians commonly offer Christ to
mankind as a nostrum to cure their ills, a way out of
their troubles, a quick and easy means to the achievement
of personal ends. They use the right words, but their
emphasis is awry. The message is so presented as to
leave the hearer with the impression that he is being
asked to give up much to gain more. H12

———

God salvages the individual by liquidating him and then
raising him again to newness of life. H44

———

Christ can and will save a man who *has been* dishonest,
but He cannot save him *while* he is dishonest. Absolute
candor is an indispensable requisite to salvation. H90

———

Mankind is still inventing new ways of self-treatment
and medication for failures and weaknesses and wrongdoing, even in our own day, not recognizing that the
cure has already come. K73

———

Jesus did not come to save learned men only. He came
to save the sinner! Not white men only—but all colors
that are under the sun. Not young people only—but
people of all ages! K75

Science and Religion

The modern scientist has lost God amid the wonders of
His world; we Christians are in real danger of losing
God amid the wonders of His Word. A13

Science, the sweet talking goddess which but a short time ago smilingly disposed of the Bible as a trustworthy guide and took the world by the hand to lead it into a man-made millennium, has turned out to be a dragon capable of destroying that same world with a flick of her fiery tail.

The world talks of peace, and by peace it means the absence of war. What it overlooks is that there is another meaning of the word, namely, tranquillity of heart, and without that kind of peace the peace of the world will continue to be but an unattainable dream. D 108

———

In recent years among certain evangelicals there has arisen a movement designed to prove the truths of Scriptures by appeal to science. Evidence is sought in the natural world to support supernatural revelation. Snowflakes, blood, stones, strange marine creatures, birds and many other natural objects are brought forward as proof that the Bible is true. This is touted as being a great support to faith, the idea being that if a Bible doctrine can be *proved* to be true, faith will spring up and flourish as a consequence.

What these brethren do not see is that the very fact that they feel a necessity to seek proof for the truths of the Scriptures proves something else altogether, namely, their own basic unbelief. H32

Self

Self is the opaque veil that hides the Face of God from us. A46

The world of sense intrudes upon our attention day and night for the whole of our lifetime. It is clamorous, insistent and self-demonstrating. It does not appeal to our faith; it is here, assaulting our five senses, demanding to be accepted as real and final. But sin has so clouded the lenses of our hearts that we cannot see that other reality, the City of God, shining around us. The world of sense triumphs. The visible becomes the enemy of the invisible; the temporal, of the eternal. [A56]

——

The desire to be held in esteem by our fellow men is universal and as natural to us as is the instinct for self-preservation. [D52]

——

The natural man is a sinner because and only because he challenges God's selfhood in relation to his own. In all else he may willingly accept the sovereignty of God; in his own life he rejects it. For him, God's dominion ends where his begins. [F36]

——

The essence of legalism is self-atonement. The seeker tries to make himself acceptable to God by some act of restitution, or by self-punishment or the feeling of regret. The desire to be pleasing to God is commendable certainly, but the effort to please God by self-effort is not, for it assumes that sin once done may be undone, an assumption wholly false. [G98]

——

Hardly anything else reveals so well the fear and uncertainty among men as the length to which they

will go to hide their true selves from each other and
even from their own eyes. G101

___

Self-knowledge is so critically important to us in our
pursuit of God and His righteousness that we lie under
heavy obligation to do immediately whatever is necessary
to remove the disguise and permit our real selves to be
known. G101

___

Rules for Self Discovery

1. *What we want most.*
2. *What we think about most.*
3. *How we use our money.*
4. *What we do with our leisure time.*
5. *The company we enjoy.*
6. *Whom and what we admire.*
7. *What we laugh at.* G103

___

Self-derogation is bad for the reason that self must be
there to derogate. Self, whether swaggering or groveling,
can never be anything but hateful to God. H71

___

Boasting is an evidence that we are pleased with self;
belittling, that we are disappointed in it. Either way we
reveal that we have a high opinion of ourselves. H71

___

The victorious Christian neither exalts nor downgrades
himself. His interests have shifted from self to Christ.

What he is or is not no longer concerns him. He believes that he has been crucified with Christ and he is not willing either to praise or deprecate such a man. H72

———

Self is one of the toughest plants that grows in the garden of life. It is, in fact, indestructible by any human means. Just when we are sure it is dead it turns up somewhere as robust as ever to trouble our peace and poison the fruit of our lives. H72

———

Christ never intended that we should rest in a mere theory of self-denial. His teaching identified His disciples with Himself so intimately that they would have had to be extremely dull not to have understood that they were expected to experience very much the same pain and loss as He Himself did. H73

———

Of all forms of deception self-deception is the most deadly, and of all deceived persons the self-deceived are the least likely to discover the fraud. H88

———

Either the Lord Jesus Christ came to bring an end of self and reveal a new life in spiritual victory, or He came to patch and repair the old self—He certainly did not come to do both! J126

———

... in that gracious day, our rejoicing will not be in the personal knowledge that He saved us from hell, but in the joyful knowledge that He was able to renew us, bringing the old self to an end, and creating within us the new man and the new self in which can be reproduced the beauty of the Son of God. [J130]

———

Think as little of yourself as you want to, but always remember that our Lord Jesus Christ thought very highly of you—enough to give Himself for you in death and sacrifice. [J138]

Service

It seems to be a significant, if not a positively ominous, thing that the words "program" and "programming" occur so frequently in the language of the church these days. [C92]

———

. . . the fast-paced, highly spiced, entertaining service of today may be a beautiful example of masterful programming—but it is not a Christian service. The two are leagues apart in almost every essential. About the only thing they have in common is the presence of a number of persons in one room. [C92]

———

. . . evangelistic and revival services in New Testament times were never divorced from worship. [C94]

———

Never do the disciples use gimmicks to attract crowds. They count on the power of the Spirit to see them

through all the way. They gear their activities to Christ
and are content to win or lose along with Him. The
notion that they should set up a "programmed" affair
and use Jesus as a kind of sponsor never so much as
entered their heads. To them Christ was everything. To
them He was the object around which all revolved; He
was, as He still is, Alpha and Omega, the beginning and
the ending. C94

———

Some churches train their greeters and ushers to smile,
showing as many teeth as possible. But I can sense that
kind of display—and when I am greeted by a man who
is smiling because he has been trained to smile, I know
I am shaking the flipper of a trained seal. K17

———

God wants to humble you and fill you with Himself
and control you so that you can become part of the
eternal work that God wants to do in the earth in your
day! K41

Sin

The fact of sin introduces a confusing element into our
thinking about God and the universe, and requires that
we suspend judgment on many things. Paul spoke of
"the mystery of iniquity," and it becomes us to accept
his inspired words as the only possible present answer
to the question of sin. The wise man will note that
the things we cannot understand have nothing to do
with our salvation. We are saved by the truth we know.
D27

Human nature tends to excesses by a kind of evil magnetic attraction. We instinctively run to one of two extremes, and that is why we are so often in error.

A proof of this propensity to extremes is seen in the attitude of the average Christian toward the devil. I have observed among spiritual persons a tendency either to ignore him altogether or to make too much of him. Both are wrong. D40

———

"The essence of sin is to will one thing," for to set our will against the will of God is to dethrone God and make ourselves supreme in the little kingdom of Mansoul. This is sin at its evil root. Sins may multiply like the sands by the seashore, but they are yet one. Sins are because sin is. F37

———

Sin has done frightful things to us and its effect upon us is all the more deadly because we were born in it and are scarcely aware of what is happening to us. G14

———

The idea that sin is modern is false. There has not been a new sin invented since the beginning of recorded history. H48

———

It is true today as it was in Bible times that the man who hates his sins too much will get into trouble with those who do not hate sin enough. H62

The holiness of God, the wrath of God and the health
of the creation are inseparably united. Not only is it
right for God to display anger against sin, but I find it
impossible to understand how He could do otherwise. H111

———

The essence of sin is rebellion against divine authority. I11

———

When God resists a man for the sins of his spirit and
attitude, a slow, inward spiritual degeneration will take
place as a signal of the judgment that has come. A
slow hardening that comes from unwillingness to yield
will result in cynicism. The Christian joy will disappear
and there will be no more fruits of the Spirit. I101

———

. . . sin does not lie in the human body. There is nothing
in the human body that is bad. Sin lies in the will of
the man and when the man wills to sin, he uses his
body as a harmless, helpless instrument to do his evil
purposes. J111

———

The holy man is not one who cannot sin. A holy man
is one who will not sin. K88

Spirituality

. . . we have been forced to look elsewhere for our
delights and we have found them in the dubious artistry
of converted opera singers or the tinkling melodies of

odd and curious musical arrangements. We have tried to secure spiritual pleasures by working upon fleshly emotions and whipping up synthetic feeling by means wholly carnal. [B81]

———

To the absence of the spirit may be traced that vague sense of unreality which almost everywhere invests religion in our times. In the average church service the most real thing is the shadowy unreality of everything. The worshipper sits in a state of suspended mentation; a kind of dreamy numbness creeps upon him; he hears words but they do not register, he cannot relate them to anything on his own life-level. He is conscious of having entered a kind of half-world; his mind surrenders itself to a more or less pleasant mood which passes with the benediction leaving no trace behind. It does not affect anything in his everyday life. He is aware of no power, no Presence, no spiritual reality. There is simply nothing in his experience corresponding to the things which he heard from the pulpit or sang in the hymns. [B90]

———

The great need of the hour among persons spiritually hungry is twofold: First, to know the Scriptures, apart from which no saving truth will be vouchsafed by our Lord; the second, to be enlightened by the Spirit, apart from whom the Scriptures will not be understood. [C37]

———

Contentment with earthly goods is the mark of a saint; contentment with our spiritual state is a mark of inward blindness. [C55]

———

Were some watcher or holy one from the bright world above to come among us for a time with the power to diagnose the spiritual ills of church people there is one entry which I am quite sure would appear on the vast majority of his reports: *Definite evidence of chronic spiritual lassitude; level of moral enthusiasm extremely low.* E7

———

When the Spirit presents Christ to our inner vision it has an exhilarating effect on the soul much as wine has on the body. The Spirit-filled man may literally dwell in a state of spiritual fervor amounting to a mild and pure inebriation. E9

———

The concept of spirituality varies among different Christian groups. In some circles the highly vocal person who talks religion continually is thought to be very spiritual; others accept noisy exuberance as a mark of spirituality, and in some churches the man who prays first, longest and loudest gets a reputation for being the most spiritual man in the assembly. G110

———

. . .a vigorous testimony, frequent prayers and loud praise may be entirely consistent with spirituality, but it is important that we understand that they do not in themselves constitute it nor prove that it is present. G112

———

True spirituality manifests itself in certain dominant desires.

1. *First is the desire to be holy rather than happy.*

2. *A man may be considered spiritual when he wants to see the honor of God advanced through his life.*

3. *The spiritual man wants to carry his cross.*

4. *Again a Christian is spiritual when he sees everything from God's viewpoint.*

5. *Another desire of the spiritual man is to die right rather than to live wrong.*

6. *The desire to see others advance at his expense.*

7. *The spiritual man habitually makes eternity-judgments instead of time-judgments.* C113

———

... if you are not punctual, you are not spiritual! J25

Theology

I sometimes fear that theology itself may exist as a semiopaque veil behind which God, if seen at all, is seen only imperfectly. Theology is precious because it is the study of God. And the very English word in its composition puts God where He belongs—first. E110

———

A man need not be godly to learn theology. Indeed I wonder whether there is anything taught in any seminary on earth that could not be learned by a brigand or a swindler as well as by a consecrated Christian. G56

Thought

A doctrine has practical value only as far as it is *prominent in our thoughts* and *makes a difference in our lives.* B65

God's thoughts belong to the world of spirit, man's to
the world of intellect, and while spirit can embrace
intellect, the human intellect can never comprehend
spirit. [B77]

———

What we think about when we are free to think about
what we will—that is what we are or will soon become. [D45]

———

... if we are honest with ourselves we can discover not
only what we are but what we are going to become.
We'll soon be the sum of our voluntary thoughts. [D46]

———

The best way to control our thoughts is to offer the
mind to God in complete surrender. [D47]

———

What comes into our minds when we think about God
is the most important thing about us. [F7]

———

... there is scarcely an error in doctrine or a failure in
applying Christian ethics that cannot be traced finally
to imperfect and ignoble thoughts about God. [F10]

———

It is not a cheerful thought that millions of us who live
in a land of Bibles, who belong to churches and labor
to promote the Christian religion, may yet pass our

whole life on this earth without once having thought or tried to think seriously about the being of God. [F34]

———

God wills that we think His thoughts after Him. [G95]

———

Our thoughts are the product of our thinking, and since these are of such vast importance to us it is imperative that we learn how to think rightly. [G95]

———

There are few emotions so satisfying as the joy that comes from the act of recognition when we see and identify our own thoughts. [H149]

———

That writer does the most for us who brings to our attention thoughts that lay close to our minds waiting to be acknowledged as our own. [H149]

———

. . . a person who is intellectually lazy is a sinful person. God had a reason for giving us our heads with intellectual capacity for thinking and reasoning and considering. But what a great company of humans there are who refuse to use their heads and many of these are Christians. [I126]

Time and Eternity

We habitually stand in our *now* and look back by faith to see the past filled with God. We look forward and see Him inhabiting our future; but our *now* is uninhabited except for ourselves. Thus we are guilty of a kind of pro tem atheism which leaves us alone in the universe while, for the time, God is not. We talk of Him much and loudly, but we secretly think of Him as being absent, and we think of ourselves as inhabiting a parenthetic interval between the God who was and the God who will be. And we are lonely with an ancient and cosmic loneliness. [B23]

——

With God Abram's day and this day are the same. [B28]

——

God is always first, and God will surely be last.

To say this is not to draw God downward into the stream of time and involve Him in the flux and flow of the world. He stands above His own creation and outside of time; but for the convenience of His creatures, who are children of time, He makes free use of time-words when referring to Himself. So He says that He is Alpha and Omega, the beginning and the ending, the first and the last. [C158]

——

God dwells in eternity but time dwells in God. He has already lived all our tomorrows as He has lived all our yesterdays. [F45]

——

That God appears at time's beginning is not too difficult to comprehend, but that He appears at the beginning and end of time *simultaneously* is not so easy to grasp. [F46]

We who live in this nervous age would be wise to meditate on our lives and our days long and often before the face of God and on the edge of eternity. For we are made for eternity as certainly as we are made for time, and as responsible moral beings we must deal with both. [F47]

———

To be made for eternity and forced to dwell in time is for mankind a tragedy of huge proportions. All within us cries for life and permanence, and everything around us reminds us of mortality and change. Yet that God has made us of the stuff of eternity is both a glory and a prophecy, a glory yet to be realized and a prophecy yet to be fulfilled. [F47]

———

How completely satisfying to turn from our limitations to a God who has none. Eternal years lie in His heart. For Him time does not pass, it remains; and those who are in Christ share with Him all the riches of limitless time and endless years. [F52]

———

God has said He will exalt you in due time, but remember, He is referring to His time and not yours! [1104]

———

As children of God, we can always afford to wait. A saint of God does not have to be concerned about time when he is in the will of God.

It is the sinner who has no time. He has to hurry or he will go to hell, but the Christian has an eternity of blessedness before him. [1104]

Tolerance and Intolerance

A new Decalogue has been adopted by the neo-Christians of our day, the first word of which reads "Thou shalt not disagree"; and a new set of Beatitudes too, which begins "Blessed are they that tolerate everything, for they shall not be made accountable for anyting." [H67]

———

The communist nations, themselves the most intolerant, are preaching and calling for tolerance in order to break down all of the borders of religion and embarrass the American people with our social and racial problems. [J123]

———

. . . the most intolerant book in all the wide world is the Bible, the inspired Word of God, and the most intolerant teacher that ever addressed himself to an audience was the Lord Jesus Christ Himself. [J123]

Tongues

I have often said to many of my friends in the groups associated with what is called "the tongues movement." I do not believe it is proper to magnify one gift above all others, particularly when that gift is one that Paul described as of least value.

I cannot believe that the unscriptural exhibition of that gift in public, like a child with a new toy, can be pleasing to God.

I believe that in any setting, the tendency to place personal feeling above the Scriptures is always an insult to God. [K26]

Trinity

God is a Trinity in Unity. [D25]

A popular belief among Christians divides the work of
God between the three Persons, giving a specific part to
each, as, for instance, creation to the Father, redemption
to the Son, and regeneration to the Holy Spirit. This
is partly true but not wholly so, for God cannot so divide
Himself that one Person works while another is inactive.
In the Scriptures the three Persons are shown to act in
harmonious unity in all the mighty works that are
wrought throughout the universe. [F31]

Trust

What we need very badly these days is a company of
Christians who are prepared to trust God as completely
now as they know they must do at the last day. For
each of us the time is surely coming when we shall
have nothing but God. Health and wealth and friends
and hiding places will all be swept away and we shall
have only God. To the man of pseudo faith that is a
terrifying thought, but to real faith it is one of the most
comforting thoughts the heart can entertain. [C50]

God constantly encourages us to trust Him in the dark. [F69]

If our faith is to have a firm foundation we must be
convinced beyond any possible doubt that God is
altogether worthy of our trust. [G26]

True faith is not the intellectual ability to visualize unseen things to the satisfaction of our imperfect minds; it is rather the moral power to trust Christ. [G70]

Truth

Divine truth is of the nature of spirit and for that reason can be received only by spiritual revelation. [B76]

———

An unblessed soul filled with the letter of truth may actually be worse off than a pagan kneeling before a fetish. [B103]

———

The uncomprehending mind is unaffected by truth. [D59]

———

Theological truth is useless until it is obeyed. The purpose behind all doctrine is to secure moral action. [E27]

———

Truth engages the citadel of the human heart and is not satisfied until it has conquered everything there. [E27]

———

As long as people can hear orthodox truth divorced from life they will attend and support churches and institutions without objection. The truth is a lovely song, become sweet by long and tender association; and since it asks nothing but a few dollars, and offers good music, pleasant friendships and a comfortable sense of well-being, it meets with no resistance from the faithful. Much that passes for New Testament Christianity is little more than objective truth sweetened with song and made palatable by religious entertainment. [E28]

———

Truth is a glorious but hard mistress. She never consults, bargains or compromises. [E39]

———

The truth is self-validating and self-renewing; its whole psychology is that of attack. Its own vigorous attack is all the defense it needs. [E97]

———

Most of us go through life praying a little, planning a little, jockeying for position, hoping but never being quite certain of anything, and always secretly afraid that we will miss the way. This is a tragic waste of truth and never gives rest to the heart. [F69]

———

Many of the doctrinal divisions among the churches are the result of a blind and stubborn insistence that truth has but one wing. [G59]

———

Unused truth becomes as useless as an unused muscle. [G59]

———

. . . truth, to be understood, must be lived; that Bible doctrine is wholly ineffective until it has been digested and assimilated by the total life. [G92]

The essence of my belief is that there is a difference, a vast difference, between fact and truth. Truth in the Scriptures is more than a fact. A fact may be detached, impersonal, cold and totally disassociated from life. Truth on the other hand, is warm, living and spiritual. A theological fact may be held in the mind for a lifetime without its having any positive effect upon the moral character; but truth is creative, saving, transforming, and it always changes the one who receives it into a humbler and holier man. [G92]

————

Not facts, not scientific knowledge, but eternal Truth delivers men, and that eternal Truth became flesh to dwell among us. *"This is life eternal, that they might know thee the only true God, and Jesus Christ, whom thou hast sent."* [H25]

————

What are the axiomatic truths upon which all human life may rest with confidence? Fortunately they are not many. Here are the chief ones:
1. *Only God is great.*
2. *Only God is wise.*
3. *Apart from God nothing matters.*
4. *Only what we do in God will remain to us at last.*
5. *Human sin is real.*
6. *With God there is forgiveness.*
7. *Only what God protects is safe.* [H116]

————

When men deal with things earthly and temporal they demand truth; when they come to the consideration

of things heavenly and eternal they hedge and hesitate
as if truth either could not be discovered or didn't matter
anyway. [H162]

——

. . . one of the greatest weaknesses in the modern church
is the willingness to lay down foundations of truth
without ever backing them up with moral application. [I120]

Victory

The degree of blessing enjoyed by any man will
correspond exactly with the completeness of God's
victory over him. [B53]

——

God is always glorified when He wins a moral victory
over us, and we are always benefited, immeasurably and
gloriously benefited. The glory of God and the everlasting
welfare of His people are always bound up together. [C117]

Will

There are two worlds, set over against each other,
dominated by two wills, the will of man and the will of
God, respectively. [B44]

——

How deeply do men err who conceive of God as subject
to our human will or as standing respectfully to wait
upon our human pleasure. Though He in condescending
love may seem to place Himself at our disposal, yet
never for the least division of a moment does He abdicate

His throne or void His right as Lord of man and nature. He is that Majesty on high. B50

____

Were God to override our wills He would be forcing Himself upon us and by so doing would make us a little less than human and so a little less than the being He made for Himself. G83

____

The dead church holds to the shell of truth without surrendering the will to it, while the church that wills to do God's will is immediately blessed with a visitation of spiritual powers. G93

____

Religion lies in the will and so does righteousness. The only good that God recognizes is a willed good; the only valid holiness is a willed holiness. H36

____

The will is the automatic pilot that keeps the soul on course. H36

____

The root of all evil in human nature is the corruption of the will. H36

____

. . . the will is master of the heart. H37

____

God has given men and women the opportunity for free will and free choices—and some are determined to have what they want most. J56

Wisdom

Let a man become enamored of Eternal Wisdom and set his heart to win her and he takes on himself a full-time, all-engaging pursuit. E39

——

There is a better way. It is to repudiate our own wisdom and take instead the infinite wisdom of God. Our insistence upon seeing ahead is natural enough, but it is a real hindrance to our spiritual progress. God has charged Himself with full responsibility for our eternal happiness and stands ready to take over the management of our lives the moment we turn in faith to Him. F69

Wonder

So many wonders have been discovered or invented that nothing on earth is any longer wonderful. Everything is common and almost everything boring. D69

——

In theology there is no "Oh!" and this is a significant if not an ominous thing. Theology seeks to reduce what may be known of God to intellectual terms, and as long as the intellect can comprehend it can find words to express itself. When God Himself appears before the mind, awesome, vast and incomprehensible, then the mind sinks into silence and the heart cries out "O Lord God!" D86

Word and Deed

As an athlete uses a ball so do many of us use words: words spoken and words sung, words written and words uttered in prayer. We throw them swiftly across the field; we learn to handle them with dexterity and grace; we build reputations upon our word-skill and gain as our reward the applause of those who have enjoyed the game. But the emptiness of it is apparent from the fact that after the pleasant religious game *no one is basically any different from what he had been before.* B32

———

... we modern Christians are long on talk and short on conduct. D32

———

We settle for words in religion because deeds are too costly. It is easier to pray, "Lord, help me to carry my cross daily" than to pick up the cross and carry it; but since the mere request for help to do something we do not actually intend to do has a certain degree of religious comfort, we are content with repetition of the words. D34

———

How then shall we escape the snare of words without deeds?

It is simple, though not easy. First, let us say nothing we do not mean. Break the habit of conventional religious chatter. Speak only as we are ready to take the consequences. Believe God's promises and obey His commandments. Practice the truth and we may with propriety speak the truth. Deeds give body to words. As we do acts of power our words will take on authority and a new sense of reality will fill our hearts. D35

———

We are moral beings and as such we must accept the consequence of every deed done and every word spoken.

We cannot act apart from the concept of right and wrong. [E47]

Work

God wants worshipers before workers; indeed the only acceptable workers are those who have learned the lost art of worship. It is inconceivable that a sovereign and holy God should be so hard up for workers that He would press into service anyone who had been empowered regardless of his moral qualifications. The very stones would praise Him if the need arose and a thousand legions of angels would leap to do His will. [G37]

———

When God put Adam and Eve in the garden, He did not put them there to sit and look at each other and to hold hands. He said they were to take care of the garden. You remember that—they were given something to do. Some people believe that work is a result of the curse, but that's not true. The idea is abroad that the man who works is a boob, and that work is only for fools— but God made us to work. [J171]

World

The Christian is called to separation from the world, but we must be sure we know what we mean (or more important, what God means) by the *world*. We are likely to make it mean something external only and thus miss its real meaning. The theatre, cards, liquor, gambling: these are not the world; they are merely an external manifestation of the world. Our warfare is not against mere worldly ways, but against the *spirit* of the world.

For man, whether he is saved or lost, is essentially spirit.
The world, in the New Testament meaning of the word,
is simply unregenerate human nature wherever it is
found, whether in a tavern or in a church. Whatever
springs out of, is built upon or receives support from
fallen human nature is the world, whether it is morally
base or morally respectable. [B117]

———

To live in a world under siege is to live in constant
peril; to live there and be wholly unaware of the peril is
to increase it a hundredfold and to turn the world into
a paradise for fools. [D42]

———

We must face today as children of tomorrow. We must
meet the uncertainties of this world with the certainty
of the world to come. To the pure in heart nothing really
bad can happen. He may die, but what is death to a
Christian? Not death but sin should be our great fear.
Without doubt the heavens being on fire shall be
dissolved, and the earth and the works that are therein
shall be burned up. Sooner or later that will come. But
what of it? Do not we, according to His promise, look
for new heavens and a new earth, wherein dwelleth
righteousness? [E131]

———

Our whole modern world is geared to destroy individual
independence and bring all of us into conformity to all
the rest of us. Any deviation from the pattern, whatever
that pattern may be at the time, will not be forgiven
by society, and since the Christian must deviate radically
from the world he naturally comes in for the world's
displeasure. [G88]

The whole world has been booby-trapped by the devil, and the deadliest trap of all is the religious one. [H84]

We still know so little about the far reaches of the universe, but as the astronomers tell us that the very Milky Way is not a milky way at all—but simply an incredible profusion of stars, billions of light-years away, and yet all moving in their prescribed and orderly directions. [J98]

It is hard to focus attention upon a better world to come when a more comfortable one than this can hardly be imagined. [H155]

If God had made all the stars in heaven according to a uniform pattern of size and distance from the earth, it would be like gazing at a glaring theater marquee rather than at the mysterious, wonderful heaven of God that we see when the skies are clear. [K109]

Worldliness

If we truly want to follow God we must seek to be other-worldly. This I say knowing well that that word has been used with scorn by the sons of this world and applied to the Christian as a badge of reproach. So be it. Every man must choose his world. [A57]

Christianity is so entangled with the world that millions never guess how radically they have missed the New Testament pattern. Compromise is everywhere. The world is whitewashed just enough to pass inspection by blind men posing as believers, and those same believers are everlastingly seeking to gain acceptance with the world. By mutual concessions men who call themselves Christians manage to get on with men who have for the things of God nothing but quiet contempt. [B111]

———

The body of evangelical believers under evil influences, has during the last twenty-five years gone over the world in complete and abject surrender, avoiding only a few of the grosser sins such as drunkenness and sexual promiscuity.

   That this disgraceful betrayal has taken place in broad daylight with full consent of our Bible teachers and evangelists is one of the most terrible affairs in the spiritual history of the world. [C109]

———

We must have a new reformation. There must come a violent break with that irresponsible, amusement-mad, paganized pseudo religion which passes today for the faith of Christ and which is being spread all over the world by unspiritual men employing unscriptural methods to achieve their ends. [C110]

———

... it has always been difficult to understand those evangelical Christians who insist upon living in the crisis as if no crisis existed. They say they serve the

Lord, but they divide their days so as to leave plenty of time to play and loaf and enjoy the pleasures of the world as well. They are at ease while the world burns; and they can furnish many convincing reasons for their conduct, even quoting Scripture if you press them a bit. D31

———

The stodgy pedestrian mind does no credit to Christianity. Let it dominate the church long enough and it will force her to take one of two directions: either toward liberalism, where she will find relief in a false freedom, or toward the world, where she will find an enjoyable but fatal pleasure. D95

———

. . . the great majority of evangelical Christians, while kept somewhat in line by the pressure of group opinion, nevertheless have a boundless, if perforce secret, admiration for the world. G103

———

The church today is suffering from the secularization of the sacred. By accepting the world's values, thinking its thoughts and adopting its ways we have dimmed the glory that shines overhead. We have not been able to bring earth to the judgment of heaven so we have brought heaven to the judgment of the earth. Pity us, Lord, for we know not what we do! H56

———

Any religious movement that imitates the world in any of its manifestations is false to the cross of Christ and on the side of the devil—and this regardless of how

192

much purring its leaders may do about "accepting Christ" or "letting God run your business." H132

———

Tolerance, charity, understanding, good will, patience and other such words and ideas are lifted from the Bible, misunderstood and applied indiscriminately to every situation. The kidnapper will not steal your baby if you only try to understand him; the burglar caught sneaking into your house with a gun is not really bad; he is just hungry for fellowship and togetherness; the gang killer taking his victim for a one-way ride can be dissuaded from committing murder if someone will only have faith in his basic goodness and have a talk with him. And this is supposed to be the teaching of Jesus, which it most certainly is not.

This yen to confer has hit the church also, which is not strange since almost everything the church is doing these days has been suggested to her by the world. H166

Worship

Men who refuse to worship the true God now worship themselves with tender devotion. B52

———

. . . never forget that it is a privilege to wonder, to stand in delighted silence before the Supreme Mystery and whisper, "O Lord God, thou knowest!" C79

———

God saves men to make them worshipers. D125

Youth

The church is called the household of God, and it is the ideal place to rear young Christians. D113

Hymns

OUT OF THE DEPTHS
(Music: Massenet's *Elegy*)

Out of the depths do I cry,
   O God, To Thee!
Hide now Thy face from my sin!
Fountains of tears flow in vain,
   So dark the stain
Tears cannot wash it away.
Bearing the shame in my heart;
Broken with anguish I mourn all the day,
Grief my companion the lonely night through.
Though I have gone far astray,
   Turn not away;
Lord, I have hoped in Thy Word.
Think on Thy mercy and rescue my soul
   Now lest I die!

High as the heavens above,
   Deep as the sea,
Lord, is Thy goodness to me.
Faithful art Thou to forgive,
   Now shall I live
To sing of Thy wonderful love.
Thou hast redeemed me,
Through grace I am Thine,
   O joy divine.
   Thine evermore.   193

194

WORD OF THE FATHER
(Music: Schubert's *Ave Maria*)

Word of the Father! Light of light;
Eternal praise is Thine alone;
Strong in Thy uncreated might,
Sweet with a holy fragrance all Thine own.
The dark beginnings of creation
Had their first rise and spring in Thee;
The universe, Thy habitation,
Which art, and evermore shalt be.
    Word of the Father!

Word of the Father! Truly God,
And truly man by incarnation,
Born to endure the thorns, the rod,
The shameful wounds for our salvation.
Our sins, our woes come all before us,
We have no friend, no friend but Thee;
O spread Thy saving mantle o'er us,
And set our mourning spirits free.
    Word of the Father!

Word of the Father! Hear our prayer!
Send far the evil tempter from us,
And make these souls Thy tender care
Lest sin and Satan overcome us.
O conquering Christ! Deep hell, despairing,
Must bow and own Thy right to reign,
When Thou, with joy beyond comparing
Shalt bring Thy ransomed ones again.
    Word of the Father!

Prayers

(from THE KNOWLEDGE OF THE HOLY)

*O Lord God Almighty, not the God of the philosophers
and the wise but the God of the prophets and apostles;
and better than all, the God and Father of our Lord
Jesus Christ, may I express Thee unblamed!*
*They that know Thee not may call upon Thee as other
than Thou art, and so worship not Thee but a creature
of their own fancy; therefore enlighten our minds that
we may know Thee as Thou art, so that we may
perfectly love Thee and worthily praise Thee.*
In the name of Jesus Christ our Lord. Amen. [9]*

———

*Lord, how great is our dilemma! In Thy Presence silence
best becomes us, but love inflames our hearts and
constrains us to speak.*
*Were we to hold our peace the stones would cry out;
yet if we speak, what shall we say! Teach us to know
that we cannot know, for the things of God knoweth
no man, but the Spirit of God. Let faith support us
where reason fails, and we shall think because we
believe, not in order that we may believe.*
In Jesus' name. Amen. [14]

Superior figure indicates page number.

O majesty unspeakable, my soul desires to behold thee.
I cry to Thee from the dust.

Yet when I inquire after Thy name it is secret. Thou are
hidden in the light which no man can approach unto.
What Thou art cannot be thought or uttered, for Thy
glory is ineffable.

Still, prophet and psalmist, apostle and saint have
encouraged me to believe that I may in some measure
know Thee. Therefore, I pray, whatever of Thyself Thou
hast been pleased to disclose, help me to search out as
treasure more precious than rubies or the merchandise
of fine gold: for with Thee shall I live when the stars
of the twilight are no more and the heavens have
vanished away and only Thou remainest. Amen.[20]

————

God of our fathers, enthroned in light, how rich, how
musical is the tongue of England! Yet when we attempt
to speak forth Thy wonders, our words how poor they
seem and our speech how unmelodious. When we
consider the fearful mystery of Thy Triune Godhead we
lay our hand upon our mouth. Before that burning bush
we ask not to understand, but only that we may fitly
adore Thee, One God in Persons Three. Amen. [25]

————

Lord of all being! Thou alone canst affirm I AM THAT
I AM; yet we who are made in Thine image may each
one repeat "I am," so confessing that we derive from
Thee and that our words are but an echo of Thine own.
We acknowledge Thee to be the great Original of which
we through Thy goodness are grateful if imperfect
copies. We worship Thee, O Father Everlasting. Amen.[32]

Teach us, O God, that nothing is necessary to Thee. Were anything necessary to Thee that thing would be the measure of Thine imperfection: and how could we worship one who is imperfect? If nothing is necessary to Thee, then no one is necessary, and if no one, then not we. Thou dost seek us though Thou dost not need us. We seek Thee because we need Thee, for in Thee we live and move and have our being. Amen.[39]

———

This day our hearts approve with gladness what our reason can never fully comprehend, even Thine eternity, O Ancient of Days. Art Thou not from everlasting, O Lord, my God, mine Holy One?

We worship Thee, the Father Everlasting, whose years shall have no end; and Thee, the love-begotten Son whose goings forth have been ever of old; we also acknowledge and adore Thee, Eternal Spirit, who before the foundation of the world didst live and love in coequal glory with the Father and the Son.

Enlarge and purify the mansions of our souls that they may be fit habitations for Thy Spirit, who dost prefer before all temples the upright heart and pure. Amen.[44]

———

Our Heavenly Father: Let us see Thy glory, if it must be from the shelter of the cleft rock and from beneath the protection of Thy covering hand. Whatever the cost to us in loss of friends or goods or length of days let us know Thee as Thou art, that we may adore Thee as we should. Through Jesus Christ our Lord. Amen.[49]

———

O Christ our Lord, Thou hast been our dwelling place in all generations. As conies to their rock, so have we run to Thee for safety; as birds from their wanderings, so have we flown to Thee for peace. Chance and change are busy in our little world of nature and men, but in Thee we find no variableness nor shadow of turning. We rest in Thee without fear or doubt and face our tomorrows without anxiety. Amen. [55]

———

Lord, Thou knowest all things; Thou knowest my downsitting and mine uprising and art acquainted with all my ways. I can inform Thee of nothing and it is vain to try to hide anything from Thee. In the light of Thy perfect knowledge I would be as artless as a little child. Help me to put away all care, for Thou knowest the way that I take and when Thou hast tried me I shall come forth as gold. Amen. [61]

———

Thou, O Christ, who wert tempted in all points like as we are, yet without sin, make us strong to overcome the desire to be wise and to be reputed wise by others as ignorant as ourselves. We turn from our wisdom as well as from our folly and flee to Thee, the wisdom of God and the power of God. Amen. [65]

———

Our Heavenly Father, we have heard Thee say, "I am the Almighty God; walk before me, and be thou perfect." But unless Thou dost enable us by the exceeding greatness of Thy power how can we who are by nature weak and sinful walk in a perfect way! Grant that we may learn to lay hold on the working of the mighty power which wrought in Christ when Thou didst raise Him from the dead and set Him at Thine own right hand in the heavenly places. Amen.[71]

O Lord our Lord, there is none like Thee in heaven
above or in the earth beneath. Thine is the greatness
and the dignity and the majesty. All that is in the heaven
and the earth is Thine; Thine is the kingdom and the
power and the glory forever, O God, and Thou art exalted
as head over all. Amen. [75]

———

Our Father, we know that Thou art present with us,
but our knowledge is but a figure and shadow of truth
and has little of the spiritual savor and inward sweetness
such knowledge should afford. This is for us a great
loss and the cause of much weakness of heart. Help us
to make at once such amendment of life as is necessary
before we can experience the true meaning of the words
"In thy presence is fulness of joy." Amen. [80]

———

It is a good thing to give thanks unto Thee and to sing
praises unto Thy name, O Most High, to show forth
Thy loving-kindness in the morning and Thy faithfulness
every night. As Thy Son while on earth was loyal to
Thee, His Heavenly Father, so now in heaven He is
faithful to us, His earthly brethren; and in this
knowledge we press on with every confident hope for
all the years and centuries yet to come. Amen. [84]

———

Do good in Thy good pleasure unto us, O Lord. Act
toward us not as we deserve but as it becomes Thee,
being the God Thou art. So shall we have nothing to
fear in this world or in that which is to come. Amen. [88]

———

Our Father, we love Thee for Thy justice. We acknowledge that Thy judgments are true and righteous

altogether. *Thy justice upholds the order of the universe
and guarantees the safety of all who put their trust in
Thee. We live because Thou art just—and merciful.
Holy, holy, holy, Lord God Almighty, righteous in all
Thy ways and holy in all Thy works. Amen.* [92]

———

*Holy Father, Thy wisdom excites our admiration, Thy
power fills us with fear, Thy omnipresence turns every
spot of earth into holy ground; but how shall we thank
Thee enough for Thy mercy which comes down to the
lowest part of our need to give us beauty for ashes, the
oil of joy for mourning, and for the spirit of heaviness a
garment of praise? We bless and magnify Thy mercy,
through Jesus Christ our Lord. Amen.* [96]

———

*God of all grace, whose thoughts toward us are ever
thoughts of peace and not of evil, give us hearts to
believe that we are accepted in the Beloved; and give
us minds to admire that perfection of moral wisdom
which found a way to preserve the integrity of heaven
and yet receive us there. We are astonished and marvel
that one so holy and dread should invite us into Thy
banqueting house and cause love to be the banner over
us. We cannot express the gratitude we feel, but look
Thou on our hearts and read it there. Amen.* [100]

———

*Our Father which art in heaven, we Thy children are
often troubled in mind, hearing within us at once the
affirmations of faith and the accusations of conscience.
We are sure that there is in us nothing that could
attract the love of One as holy and as just as Thou art.
Yet Thou hast declared Thine unchanging love for us*

in Christ Jesus. If nothing in us can win Thy love, nothing in the universe can prevent Thee from loving us. Thy love is uncaused and undeserved. Thou art Thyself the reason for the love wherewith we are loved. Help us to believe the intensity, the eternity of the love that has found us. Then love will cast out fear; and our troubled hearts will be at peace, trusting not in what we are but in what Thou hast declared Thyself to be. Amen. [104]

———

Glory be to God on high. We praise Thee, we bless Thee, we worship Thee, for Thy great glory. Lord, I uttered that I understood not; things too wonderful for me which I knew not. I heard of Thee by the hearing of the ear, but now mine eye seeth Thee and I abhor myself in dust and ashes. O Lord, I will lay my hand upon my mouth. Once have I spoken, yea, twice, but I will proceed no further.

But while I was musing the fire burned. Lord, I must speak of Thee, lest by my silence I offend against the generation of Thy children. Behold, Thou hast chosen the foolish things of the world to confound the wise, and the weak things of the world to confound the mighty. O Lord, forsake me not. Let me show forth Thy strength into this generation and Thy power to everyone that is to come. Raise up prophets and seers in Thy Church who shall magnify Thy glory and through Thine almighty Spirit restore to Thy people the knowledge of the holy. Amen. [110]

———

Who wouldst not fear Thee, O Lord God of Hosts, most high and most terrible? For Thou art Lord alone. Thou hast made heaven and the heaven of heavens, the earth *and all things that are therein, and in Thy hand is the soul of every living thing. Thou sittest king upon the flood; yea, Thou sittest king forever. Thou art a great king over all the earth. Thou art clothed with strength; honor and majesty are before Thee. Amen.*[115]

Prayers

(from THE PURSUIT OF GOD)

O God, I have tasted Thy goodness, and it has both satisfied me and made me thirsty for more. I am painfully conscious of my need of further grace. I am ashamed of my lack of desire. O God, the Triune God, I want to want Thee; I long to be filled with longing; I thirst to be made more thirsty still. Show me Thy glory, I pray Thee, that so I may know Thee indeed. Begin in mercy a new work of love within me. Say to my soul, "Rise up, my love, my fair one, and come away." Then give me grace to rise and follow Thee up from this misty lowland where I have wandered so long. In Jesus' name. Amen. [20]

——

Father, I want to know Thee, but my cowardly heart fears to give up its toys. I cannot part with them without inward bleeding, and I do not try to hide from Thee the terror of the parting. I come trembling, but I do come. Please root from my heart all those things which I have cherished so long and which have become a very part of my living self, so that Thou mayest enter and dwell there without a rival. Then shalt Thou make the place of Thy feet glorious. Then shall my heart have no need of the sun to shine in it, for Thyself wilt be the light of it, and there shall be no night there. In Jesus' name, Amen.[30]

Lord, how excellent are Thy ways, and how devious and dark are the ways of man. Show us how to die, that we may rise again to newness of life. Rend the veil of our self-life from the top down as Thou didst rend the veil of the Temple. We would draw near in full assurance of faith. We would dwell with Thee in daily experience here on this earth so that we may be accustomed to the glory when we enter Thy heaven to dwell with Thee there. In Jesus' Name, Amen.[47]

———

O God, quicken to life every power within me, that I may lay hold on eternal things. Open my eyes that I may see; give me acute spiritual perception; enable me to taste Thee and know that Thou art good. Make heaven more real to me than any earthly thing has ever been. Amen.[59]

———

O God and Father, I repent of my sinful preoccupation with visible things. The world has been too much with me. Thou hast been here and I knew it not. I have been blind to Thy presence. Open my eyes that I may behold Thee in and around me. For Christ's sake, Amen.[71]

———

Lord, teach me to listen. The times are noisy and my ears are weary with the thousand raucous sounds which continuously assault them. Give me the spirit of the boy Samuel when he said to Thee, "Speak, for thy servant heareth." Let me hear Thee speaking in my heart. Let me get used to the sound of Thy voice, that its tones may be familiar when the sounds of earth die

204

*away and the only sound will be the music of Thy
speaking voice. Amen.* [82]

———

*O Lord, I have heard a good word inviting me to look
away to Thee and be satisfied. My heart longs to
respond, but sin has clouded my vision till I see Thee
but dimly. Be pleased to cleanse me in Thine own
precious blood, and make me inwardly pure, so that I
may with unveiled eyes gaze upon Thee all the days of
my earthly pilgrimage. Then shall I be prepared to
behold Thee in full splendor in the day when Thou shalt
appear to be glorified in Thy saints and admired in all
them that believe. Amen.* [97]

———

*O God, be Thou exalted over my possessions. Nothing
of earth's treasures shall seem dear unto me if only
Thou art glorified in my life. Be Thou exalted over my
friendships. I am determined that Thou shalt be above
all, though I must stand deserted and alone in the midst
of the earth. Be Thou exalted above my comforts.
Though it mean the loss of bodily comforts and the
carrying of heavy crosses, I shall keep my vow made
this day before Thee. Be Thou exalted over my
reputation. Make me ambitious to please Thee even if
as a result I must sink into obscurity and my name be
forgotten as a dream. Rise, O Lord, into Thy proper
place of honor, above my ambitions, above my likes
and dislikes, above my family, my health and even my
life itself. Let me decrease that Thou mayest increase;
let me sink that Thou mayest rise above. Ride forth
upon me as Thou didst ride into Jerusalem mounted
upon the humble little beast, a colt, the foal of an ass,
and let me hear the children cry to Thee, "Hosanna
in the highest."* [107]

Lord make me childlike. Deliver me from the urge to compete with another for place or prestige or position. I would be simple and artless as a little child. Deliver me from pose and pretense. Forgive me for thinking of myself. Help me to forget myself and find my true peace in beholding Thee. That Thou mayest answer this prayer I humble myself before Thee. Lay upon me Thy easy yoke of self-forgetfulness that through it I may find rest. Amen.[116]

———

Lord, I would trust Thee completely; I would be altogether Thine; I would exalt Thee above all. I desire that I may feel no sense of possessing anything outside of Thee. I want constantly to be aware of Thy overshadowing presence and to hear Thy speaking voice. I long to live in restful sincerity of heart. I want to live so fully in the Spirit that all my thoughts may be as sweet incense ascending to Thee and every act of my life may be an act of worship. Therefore I pray in the words of Thy great servant of old, "I beseech Thee so for to cleanse the intent of mine heart with the unspeakable gift of Thy grace, that I may perfectly love Thee and worthily praise Thee." And all this I confidently believe Thou wilt grant me through the merits of Jesus Christ Thy Son. Amen.[127]

Anthology compiled from the following A.W.Tozer works:

Index